THE FUTURE OF
HUMAN HISTORY

THE FUTURE OF HUMAN HISTORY

Through the Possible Past
Towards a Possible Future

JAGMOHAN DYAL SINGH

PARTRIDGE
A Penguin Random House Company

To order additional copies of this book, contact
Partridge India
000 800 10062 62
orders.india@partridgepublishing.com

www.partridgepublishing.com/india

Evolution of Homo sapiens

Life on Earth has changed in quality and quantity; the day evolution mutated some creature to walk upright. Live the way we do in groups. In addition, think the way we do as selfish beings. The day nature brought forth a creature designed to kill the way we do for need as well as for pleasure, because none before it killed for pleasure. This event took place around 200,000 years ago, according to researchers.

Animal life, before human existence meant to carry itself, produce and die but human intelligence changed all that. Humans made life difficult for the rest of the living world and for their own selves. Not only are the other species at a great danger from humans, they needed to control their own kind from harming one another.

Human race wants to continue and produce, but it also wants to control others before it dies and withers away. In its possession, human race wants land and other beings that are according to it much less devised. Human race wants these less 'evolved' creatures to work as drudges and pander the humans in form of pets. The way evolution has designed humans' 'genetic makeup', the Homo sapiens also wants possession over other Homo sapiens that it considers inferior. It is no doubt a unique creature, even if created by God and not by the long trials and errors of evolution.

Humans are the only multicellular organisms that have exploited nearly all the other living organisms that they have faced, be it microbes, plants or animals. Nevertheless, the human nature of exploitation does not stop at other species. They have exploited their similar humans through lies and deceit, or through laws and unjust measures.

While animals are not subject to any laws on crime, marriage or ownership it is not that they have destroyed themselves from the face of this planet, that their society is disorderly or finishing it. Animals are safe from each other because nature has not cursed them with the use of weapons. They have not yet devised methods to harm each other by means other than the ones provided by nature.

Human hand has evolved to grip the club, the sword, and the gun. Human mind is capable of inventing weapons that can waste vast tracts of land or maybe oceans too. Therefore, to protect itself from its own self, human race developed laws. These laws became political systems as human population grew. Hence, to keep the social evolution of humans orderly their society has developed different political systems on different continents.

Due to certain discrepancies, political systems are at clash within themselves. Political systems are at war with each other too. Although many political systems have evolved through the generations and many have faded into the past. Some of them have remained to exist in the present. A day shall come when only one political system shall eventually survive on the planet, that too after destroying other political systems through war.

Political systems are creation of different races. In addition, different human races prefer to practice a specific political system. When only one political system shall eventually survive on the planet, it shall also make one specific race the representative of humans on Earth. Other races shall become extinct or be assimilated into this one race.

Human society, despite, being subject to laws, is getting disorderly in some places while remaining orderly in some. The ruling class misuse laws in many places according to their benefit. Because of this human society is on the brink of extinction with a touch of a button. It is also responsible for the extinction of many other species and one day might be responsible for destroying this planet. This proves that humans have much neglect for laws that they themselves have listed to protect their civilization and for a secure future of their children.

Although human thought has love for destruction and it has always followed its heart for the sake of its love. Yet life has a way to triumph over all the blocks put in the way of its progress. Devastation has always given way to prosperity. For human thought also has love for development, for science and for creativity. Humanity has wanted for progress and in equality for all, in pursuit of advancement of its culture and in aiming for the policy of world peace.

If some humans have promoted destruction as a tool for satisfying their demons, others have toiled in their laboratories to solve the mysteries of nature. Some have depicted the world through their creativity. Others have provided the needy with their compassion. Many have provided the world with their vision to develop into a society that promotes technological innovations to reduce drudgery and physical labour. Humans have a great potential, both in the fields of destruction and vitality. However, liveliness and growth have always outpaced destruction in human history.

Human evolution is different from other organisms. No organism on Earth has the power to change the geological presence of any ecosystem. Neither does any species have the power to deplete resources, provided by nature for the upkeep of different flora and fauna.

Humans for the sake of increasing their numbers and for the nourishment of their ever-growing population have indulged in acts that are impossible to think about in the animal world. Agriculture and animal husbandry is a great leap in the evolution of humans and for increasing their members. However, these activities, carried out by the humans have changed the planet. These human deeds caused the demise of much diversity that nature has created over the centuries.

It could be possible that by promoting such activities through the great length of past time because of their presence on this planet, humans are in fact not destroying the planet. They are in fact making it more suitable and adaptable for their future generations and for the plants and animals that are responsible for the survival of human race, as a whole. One thing is definite that the arrival of humans, on the planet has made the natural system susceptible to change through the actions of this animal. Due to their behaviour and their interaction with the environment, humans cannot be another beast among the animals but a being beyond their level of existence.

Has the evolutionary process faltered in creating the human? Who has enslaved the plants and animals, when given the opportunity enslaved its own kind for selfish gains. Used according to his will, the life of other organisms. Humanity has imprisoned other living things to quell the hunger of his stomach and to work as drudges for the human enterprise. Humanity has exposed beasts and men alike, to suffer atrocities even while providing for human growth and development.

Has evolution provided the humans with the thought process that they have a supreme authority over the planet? Humans think they can change the planet and its flora and fauna according to their desires and whims. Has evolution permitted humans to change the contours of the Earth and crater into its belly to extract all the mineral wealth that the Earth stores inside it for stabilizing its structure? In doing all the damage to the Earth for fulfilling its own needs, is humanity through the ages not upsetting the natural balance? Moreover, as human civilization grows immense with knowledge of science, it is trying to change the entire balance that nature had maintained for the upkeep of its organisms. In addition, in doing so, is humanity in fact not doing so much damage to the environment of this planet that is beyond repair and one day might just crumble and wither away?

The planet can no longer withstand human thrusts of destruction and might revert to its original form of continuation. Turn back to the time when it sustained its entire species without human presence and human interference.

While the humans, right from their origin on this world started to pace towards their impending doom, that is their own creation and will. The future of Earth in the coming ages is in the hands of humanity. Because evolution has placed it in a position where it has mastery over all the other species present on this planet. Humanity is blessed; it has the power to protect the environment from its own greed and its follies. The curse of humans is the endowment with power to extinguish the flame of survival, not only of other species, but also of its own.

Humans have tried to prevent their extinction by devising methods to govern the societies that make up Human Civilization. All social groups have chosen different methods to govern themselves. Some methods rendered obsolete by the test of time and others favoured by the experiments, carried through the ages. However, through time, as these societies try to enforce their will upon each other mainly for gaining control over resources, their methods have brought further destruction upon the world. Societies that have managed their internal social setups with insight have triumphed over the ones left to neglect and rot by the decision makers of those social setups. At times human societies have tried to obliterate each other from the face of the planet. At times, through diplomatic solutions, they have devised ways to put away stand offs. Nevertheless, societies populated by enlightened and wise people have consumed mismanaged societies. When such social setups escaped destruction created by their own follies, the superior society takes over it.

Human societies have grown from the miniscule villages and tribes into large nations and so have their needs. Some nations have inherent capabilities to outshine others. They outpace other not due to their natural resources but due to their population and the decisions that these populations make. These decisions shall be important in the near future for the protection of their individual societies and the upkeep of the planet as a whole, if the humans are to survive.

Humans shall remain the master of this planet, unless some evolutionary mechanism overthrows the supremacy of humanity by a chance mutation and change the course of human history.

HUMAN HISTORY AND EVOLUTION OF GOVERNANCE

Understanding human history is very important, if to understand the development of different human governance methods. Only history can give a good understanding about which type of governance methods are better and which are regressive for the society. As humans evolved and later diversified into many different races and cultures. They went through changes both political and social. These political and social changes took some races and societies out of their tribal setup. It directed these social groups with innovation in governance towards a higher form of social organisation. At the same time, some societies never left their tribal organisation. In addition, decided not to reach for higher levels of social developments.

Among those cultures, that reached higher levels of social organisations, are the ones utilized diversified methods to increase their power, both military and economic. Some opted for systems that involved all people for the growth of society. Powerful people or sections superimposed their will on society in other systems of governance and supressed common people.

Throughout human history, all political systems practised on this planet have clashed with each other. However, political systems have disagreed within their own selves too. As human history progressed, some systems progressed too quickly from others because they were at some inherent advantage. Slowly and steadily, the systems at an advantage consumed the disadvantaged systems and spread through human civilization. Alternatively, the superior systems destroyed the inferior, mismanaged systems.

After humans came out of the tribal organisation and constructed large human settlements. The two main political systems that prevailed on the world map were authoritative political systems and democratic political systems. When the human history was in its infancy, very few civilizations opted for the democratic political systems. Authoritative political systems were the favoured form of governments during the earlier parts of history.

Constant human immigrations, especially from the colder climates into the hotter regions and from the Northern hemisphere into the Southern hemisphere favoured this type of government. The immigrants who were fair skinned established kingdoms and empires in the warmer, Southern regions of the world and ruled over the dark skinned people already settled in these regions. Since this produced a master-slave relationship. It carried on for many centuries, where few humans could live off the toil of others through implementation of taxes.

In Europe, which produced most immigration waves from it to other parts of the globe, some civilisations practiced democracy during ancient times. It was possible for these civilizations to practise democracy because they had a belief in equality. Only because they looked alike and were from the same race, this form of government was possible. Nevertheless, the circumstances of historical times did not favour democracy as a preferred form of government because the force of arms easily subjugated populations. Villages, towns and cities could be butchered altogether if any resisted the victorious armies. Hence, slowly, even in Europe, democratic institutions gave way to authoritative governments.

Human evolution is not just the evolution of bodily change but change of social development as well. Hence as the human body changed, so did its mind and its need to change the governance of its society. However, this evolution in social change, this very important social development only threw up in Europe. In Europe, the collective strength of the ordinary human population overwhelmed the armies that subjugated societies and lived off their hard work. Hence, a democracy, a form of government in which people decide how they be governed, taxed and make decisions on their future and of their coming generations is a mutation. This mutation, like the fair-skinned mutation is the product of the European continent. In other parts of the world, no other race or society even thought about this type of governance. There is neither on record nor on any literature written by any Eastern authority on this type of governance. Democracy is a concept that is out of the scope of the Eastern societies. It is an invention of the Western world.

In the comparison of two forms of governments, both the authoritative and democratic types, the democratic type of governance is much superior to the former. It is due to this form of governance that European nations advanced their culture and their race to far corners of the world. It was due to this governance that they achieved military superiority and have the distinction of extinguishing many primitive races in the new worlds. Only due to this type of political system, the Caucasian race has raced past other races, leaving them far behind on the scale of human social evolution.

Even in democratic types of governments the federal types, which are much localised in administration are superior to the centralised ones. Hence, democratic governments too have evolved according to geographical locations, the federal or localised Western types, and the authoritative Eastern types.

To understand the superiority of one political system over the other it is important to go through human history. Although it is not important to go through the voluminous past but a few important events that can help us understand this concept. That is presented below, a few excerpts through history to make the reader understand political systems designed by humans. Which system is better and what changes are possible in the future of human history can easily made out from historical events. From these events, the outline of the future of human history to project the future of human social change is easy. It is also possible to predict with some accuracy what shall befall some societies and which social setups, for managing their organisation with care and diligence shall reap rewards.

Spreading Around the Globe

Human history division is between various periods and timelines. Some have divided human history between prehistory and history. Prehistory a period that began when human was as much a savage as it is now but could not make use of the tools of intellect that had empowered it during the times called historical periods. During the historical times, among others things human began to record his doings in pictures and words and build in monuments.

Human prehistory is very interesting indeed, for it is during the prehistory that humanity spread to every nook and corner of this planet. Eventually humans became the planet's dominant species. Hence, the prehistory of humans has shaped their history. Prehistory has decided the way of present running in human society and what the future might happen to be, for humans.

If humans are a work of evolutionary process that is same for all living things. If humans are not a part of some divine intervention or are not part of some extra-terrestrial experiment. Then most certainly the mutations that took place among the progenitors of modern humans occurred near the equatorial lines. It is where cosmic rays strike the most on the Earth's surface.

In addition, along with other forces that promote evolutionary changes, selection pressures among species and inside species, ecological and geological changes are also important. However, genetic mutations through translocations of genes on chromosomes and mutations through radiation play an important role, the most crucial role. Cosmic rays play the most important role in mutation of genes. Radiating from the sun or from the stars, it did have much to do with the presence of modern humans. A constant bombardment of cosmic rays is much more prevalent and more consistent on the equator. It is a place more likely to breed mutations than any other place on Earth and change the genetic locations and its chemical composition in any living system. The cumulative effect of these mutations through the centuries, on the equatorial line is more likely to bring forth evolutionary changes in a species, than on any other latitude on the globe.

If the scientists have hypothesised that first humans originated around 200,000 years ago on the African continent they might be correct. Nevertheless, it can be added that the first humans, no matter, on which continent they might have originated, that continent existed on the equatorial plane at one time. This means that the first humans, because they originated on the equatorial plane were, for sure, dark skinned. For the environment in which they came forth into existence, was quite sunny and hot.

The first modern human form, most probably, was the Austroloid form. This form represented by most of the tribes of the Southern Pacific and Indian Ocean Islands. This human race was abundant on the Australian continent. This human form presently found in the Indian Sub-Continent too, but in a highly mixed form. All darker races, including the Negroid races of Africa derived from this form due to development in isolated environment. This Austroloid form spread into the European continent too. The European human are most probably a mutant of this human race. This race was abundant on the entire world except the Sub Saharan Africa before the advent of the Caucasian and Mongloid humans. Until this race was driven back into the South, both by the Caucasian race and the Mongoloid population. Although it has lost presence in the Northern parts of Asia, it has a small fragment left in its Southern parts. This race survived in the remote islands and the Australian Continent. All the other human races have mutated one or the other way from this human form. It was later on that the fair skinned Caucasians or similarly mutated Mongloid populations displaced this race in the Northern parts of Asia and completely from North Africa and Europe.

As the humans began to proliferate around their surroundings and spread farther away from their original birthplace. Therefore, so did differences arise in the weather of Earth? Moreover, when humans spread farther apart from their original home, the climate of the planet changed. This changing climate served to separate the various human tribes because it produced natural barriers between human populations. At some places, vast forests came up to prevent human interaction. Thick sheets of ice covered large tracts of land during the glaciations of the ice age. Shallow seas and deep gorges were created during the recession of the glaciers called inter glaciations.

The ice age commenced just after the origin of humans. The ice age last hypothesized to have taken place between 110,000 to 12,000 years ago. It had a major role to play in later human mutations. Ice age is responsible for most human discrepancies that are visible and those that are inconspicuous to the human eye. The environment produces differences in appearances of species and humans are no different. Humans visualize and realize the differences within their species and differentiate, based on races or appearances. Other creatures are not that 'racists'. However, the various sub species that were present during the origin of humans might also have contributed to the diversity of human races. Caucasian, Mongoloid, Negroid, Negrito, Austroloid, Proto-Austroloid, and all the other minor races, at least some of them, are indeed a mixture of some human sub species.

During the ice ages, when the glaciers covered vast stretches of land under their weight. Human populations remained isolated from each other effectively during this time. Separations of great distances and for great centuries existed. This diversity was great enough to put enough bio chemical differences in the physical and chemical makeup of their bodies.

The humans that lived in the warm climates during the ice age retained their dark skins and broad noses. Their bodies secreted melatonin to protect against the ultraviolet radiation of the sun. Many other differences also arose in their morphology and biochemistry. The environment of the places covered under glaciers during the ice ages nearly always remained covered under the clouds, receiving negligible sunlight. Due to this reason, the dark skinned humans in the populations that lived in that climate started leaving less dark skinned progeny and left more light-skinned children. The environment eventually favoured light-skinned progeny. As light skins, absorbed light filtered the through clouds easily. It gave an inherent advantage to the light-skinned humans over their dark skinned brothers and sisters. In time, all dark skinned people died out due to selective pressures and only light-skinned progeny survived to spread their seed and grow their families. At certain places, certain humans mixed with certain other sub species related to humans and capable of interbreeding with humans. Hence, this mixing brought more diversity into the gene pool of the human species.

The diversity of humans into various races has also provided for diversity in the thinking patterns of different races. All biochemical and morphological changes also induce physiological changes. The chemicals that flow in the bodies of humans create these physiological changes. These chemicals make organisms think on different lines and in different directions. This applies to the different races and subdivisions of humans. Different human races have diverse chemicals in their bodies that set them apart from each other. These chemicals are responsible for the thinking pattern of an individual and of the different human races. If the humans developed different cultures and modes of governments, the different chemicals in different human races influenced such decisions.

It was the inter play of many forces, geological, ecological, mutational and breeding pressures that made humans what they are and how they behave. Moreover, what their future shall probably be, because of what they have become due to natural selection is important to overall human social development.

THE HUMAN MIGRATION

Tracing human migration from its origin shall not be difficult if not all that accurate and precise. However, a theory developed on an individual basis by a thinker for others to judge is a right method for deducing the human development. No one is certain what happened in the past. There are only glimpses through which one can peep. Until date, all we can do is hypothesize and that is all we can do in the near future until time travel is possible. From its equatorial home Homo sapiens radiated towards the North, the South and towards the longitudes. Much of the land mass from the point of humans' origin lay towards the North. There was no dearth on the South too and hence opportunities lay everywhere for the humans to exploit.

From the equator, the humans made their way into the European continent and The Central Asian Steppes and into Siberia. One branch moved through the Siberian region and finally into the fertile basins of China and down through the dense forest into South East Asia. Some during the ice ages crossed into the 'New Worlds' of the Americas, both north and South. Many branches spread throughout the Middle East and North Africa, The Iranian Plateau, Lower South Eastern Central Asian Plateau. Some went further down and settled on the islands, in between, the Asian continent and the Australian Land Mass. and from these people, some eventually reached Australia too. Mainland Africa too had its share in the movements of human migrations and humans came to spread evenly in the 'Dark Continent, too.

Human migration is a constant phenomenon; it is continuous in the movements of humans. The early migrations were responsible for the radiation of humans in all directions and these human movements have a special significance in the evolution of the human society. These migrations induced certain changes in the bodies and minds of humans inhabiting lands far from the humans' place of origin. These made the same people; with the same origin develop differently from one another not only in shape but also inside the mind.

Two forces of the ice age were responsible for developing the human race into its modern form. The glaciation periods and inter glaciation periods of the ice age. Moreover, that because they condensed and released water during their cycling and created conditions sometimes favourable and at times unfavourable for human migration.

It is possible that before the evolution of Homo sapiens, another sub species of Homo evolved some 300,000 years or so before the Homo sapiens. That was the Homo sapiens neanderthalensis. This sub species radiated out towards the North, especially towards the colder climates.

As Homo sapiens ventured into the Northern hemispheres, the Neanderthals started to disappear. Maybe due to wide scale massacre or due to some other competitive edge that Homo sapiens displayed over their less evolved or less competitive cousins Homo sapiens neanderthalensis. Most probably, the earlier humans were of the Austroloid race. It is from this race that all other races have evolved. These were the first humans to propagate around the world. During the time of Neanderthals, the modern humans looked like the aboriginal people of Australia or the nearby islands.

However, it can also be possible that as humans pushed up towards the North Pole the Neanderthals retreated further back north and east. It can also be thinkable that our ancestors probably pushed them out of Europe before the coming of the intermittent ice age towards the Siberian edge. Finally, when the ice age created a bridge of ice between the Americas and the Siberian landmasses, it was possible to cross back and forth into both the continents. The Neanderthals crossed into the new territory. This at the time was devoid of the new animal that nature had thrown into the tournament of life 'The Human'. Finding the niche empty in the Siberia, the modern humans occupied it. Eventually they too crossed over to the new continents that were devoid of the humans, as is human nature to explore into the unknown. Nevertheless, this land mass had a small population of Homo sapiens neanderthalensis that the Homo sapiens had routed from the Old World.

Moreover, when the inter glacier period set in during the ice age and the glaciers melted, all those who had crossed over, be it Neanderthals or Humans could not find their way back. It is possible that on the new continent a lot of admixture between the Humans and the Neanderthals took place. With Human blood being predominant as Humans were no doubt at an advantage at hunting and planning over their Neanderthal cousins. Nevertheless, that does not mean that the Neanderthals were not having natural advantages or that they were buffoons meant to be servile to the Homo sapiens. It is just that their pattern of thinking and their genetic makeup was a bit different from the humans slightly, only very slightly.

It could be possible, although it can never be proved in any way what so ever, that the Mongoloid people might have developed on the American continent. As some Humans who might have crossed over into the new world via the Siberian-Alaskan Route during the first Ice Age intermixed with remnants of the Neanderthals. When the ice bridge melted, their link with the old world cut off and they had to survive on the new continent. Maybe, they were not enough in numbers and that they developed quite independently, possibly with lots of admixture with the Neanderthal population. The Neanderthal population that been displaced by the Homo sapiens from the old world and were pushed into the new world had already established themselves in the new world in large numbers. Eventually these people developed a unique culture in the American continent that was very distinct from the Eurasian and African land mass.

The Mongloid people have a tendency to deposit carotene under their skins; their skulls are more gracile than other races. They are a recent development in Human evolutionary history. This suggests their evolution to be recent or latest among the human races, most possibly a hybrid between races or sub species.

At the start of the ice age, the humans that had moved into Europe, the Central Asian Steppes, and Parts of Eastern Russia were the most effected. The harsh climatic conditions made interactions among communities quite difficult and it was a hindrance for migration of humans. On top of that, the low amount of sunlight had its toll on the dark skinned people so that these people developed very fair skin, light coloured hair, and light sensitive iris of the eyes. Hence having varied eye colours present among these populations. These humans due to certain mutations became quite different from the humans of the warmer regions. The mutations induced certain chemical changes in these humans so that they thought on different lines than their progenitors.

The people living in the warmer places might have remained much the same as they were from the time, they originated. If they did mutate further, their evolution rates were supressed compared to the mutated humans in the colder climates. The darker races, all of them, most probably originated from the Austroloid race that inhabited the entire world before the coming of the ice age.

When the glaciers receded and somewhat softened the frost of the ice age the populations from Europe and other Northern Hemispheres started moving into the interior of Asia. Lots of interbreeding among populations might have taken place because human migration takes place from colder regions into the hotter regions. Many wars too might have taken place, with many deaths and massacres. Maybe obliterations of populations too might have taken place. The result was that the Asian and North African Populations got lot of admixture in their blood and it showed in their skin colour. This colour became intermediate between the two, a mix of the dark and the light complexions.

Nevertheless, the culture of this society, had the ruling class making their way through the colder climates into the warmer regions as invaders, used to harsh climates and inhospitable conditions of life. Natural selection designed this race for war. Aggression was part of their culture, a quality infused in them by their environment. The original inhabitants were hunters and gathers not wanting war, averse to the idea of conquest, living in the land of plenty and content with the bounty that nature had provided them.

Hence the over a long period in these locations, the ruling class was fair skinned and their subjects and slaves, dark skinned. However, since nature serves the purpose of union and bringing out a balance. Long interaction between the two populations finally made the local population a mixture of the two. The population in North Africa, Northern Asia, especially in upper North being a bit fairer then their Southern cousins.

The Northern parts of Africa and Asia had received more invaders from the colder parts of Europe. Many dark skinned people might have lost their lives in the wars that had taken place during possession of land from one tribe by the other and reduced the population of dark skinned people. Before this effect could reach farther into the interior of Africa and Southern Asia, another glaciation period of Ice age had set in. This time it set in for a great number of years. It also allowed the Mongoloid people to make their way back into the old world through the same route they had spread into the new world. Beyond the Urals, the Mongoloid people who came into the old world from the new world found a Caucasian population inhabiting the snow clad lands. The Mongoloid tribes would have had a lot of admixture with the local population.

Eventually after a long, time the glaciers of the times, receded. The link between the old world and the new world was broken again. Two worlds were again unknown to each other, this probably happened around 12,000 years ago.

CREATION OF RACES

Human migration after the recession of glaciers of the great ice age after 10, 000 BC is of great interest and importance in shaping human history. The world of today is resting on the foundations laid during movements that man made during this time, as population grew and so did the need to possess as much Earth as possible.

As the glaciers spread out by the ice age crept back towards the North Pole, they did their part in segregation of human races. The glaciers separated Eurasia (Europe, Northern Part of Central Asian Steppes, and Russia until the Ural Mountains) from the Siberia and China at the Ural Mountains by a shallow water body. This sea spread over the Gobi Desert and the centre of Central Asian Grasslands and then turned west and rained into the Mediterranean Sea and South into the Arabian Sea.   This sea also separated North Africa, Central Middle East, Southern Part of Central Asia, and South Asia from Siberia, Mainland China, and Southeast Asia. This sea also separated Eurasia from the Middle East, Southern Central Asia, Eastern Central Asia, and The Far East as it flowed into the Mediterranean Sea and into the Arabian Sea. North Africa too separated from Sub Saharan Africa or the interior of the continent by a shallow water body at what is now most probably, the Sahara Desert.

In short, North Africa, Western Asia and Southern Central Asia, North Western South Asia was one land mass. One particular racial group with a sea to the South and a sea and mountains to the east inhabited Europe and North Western Central Asia until the Western side of the Ural Mountains. Siberia, Mainland China, and Southeast Asia connected each other with no water barrier in between them to stop human migration. A sea extended from the Mediterranean Sea right until the middle of the central Asian steppes. A great water reservoir separated Europe from North Africa, Near East, South Asia. This also separated Europe and Western Asia from Siberia, China Mainland, and South East Asia. A shallow sea separated interior of the 'Dark Continent' from North African shores. These seas have dried up or filled up with sediments, ages ago, but have left their remnants inside the soils of the lands that they once subdued.

The American continent as has already been mentioned separated from the Europe-Asia-Africa land mass, most probably at the Bering Strait. The people living in the Eurasian land mass, could in theory, only interbreed among themselves. The population of this place has fair and ruddy skin, with eyes having coloured, light sensitive irises, and light absorbing wavy hair because the climatic conditions favoured such physical traits. It is so because these populations experienced conditions of low ultra violet radiations during the ice ages. Hence, the environmental conditions have through the centuries and through the generations favoured certain genetic mixtures. These makeups made their existence optimum in these particular conditions.

The land mass of North Africa, Near East, Iranian Plateau, Southern Central Asia and North Western South Asia was interconnected. The humans that dwelled in these parts interacted among one another. Hence, these populations are quite a lot alike each other with subtle differences and maybe during these times were quite darker than they are at present. A shallow water body in the South Asian Sub-Continent at what is now the Gangetic Plain into the east cut off this particular population's expansion further towards the east. Its expansion was restricted towards China Mainland by the Himalayan Mountains, the other mountain ranges in its vicinity altogether called the Pamir Knot. Moreover, of course, by the shallow water body in the Central Asia that extended until Eurasia and blockaded human movement. The barriers that extended from the Middle East and Southern Central Asia up Until China Mainland made immigration impossible to happen from Western Asia towards the Eastern part of the continent or vice versa.

The Mongloid People who had made their way back through the Bering Strait after the glaciation period and after they mixed with the local Caucasian population, developed some differences from their American cousins. They had fairer skins due to their mixture with the Caucasian people already present on the Siberian lands. In time, they spread down from Siberia towards the Mainland China and from its river valleys downwards through Burma and Vietnam and spread through the entire South East Asia, already occupied by the Austroloid People. Nevertheless, through destruction and assimilation the Mongloid people did have ascendency over the Austroloid people. The Austroloids pushed further down the islands towards Australia. They made for the unknown places in the South. Some reached the Australian land mass during this time. Some tribes developed societies isolated from rest of the humankind on small off shore ecosystems. They remained primitive in their social behaviours and protected by the remoteness of their abodes.

The Austroloid people also inhabited the lower part of the South Asian Sub-Continent. Nevertheless, they were not touched yet. The water bodies that served as a barrier in those days were great enough to serve as a tool of racial segregation. They let these people develop independently. These barriers protected these people from other militarily advanced races.

In the African heartland, the Negroid and the Negrito populations too remained untouched by the other human populations due to the water barriers that existed on their North and the oceans around their continent. This remoteness hindered their development by cutting them from competition with other people. Competition that is very essential for progress.

The humans on the American Continent made their way down from Alaska right down to the southernmost tip of the South America without any human resistance. They developed on very different lines from other human races that were competing and killing each other in a cut throat competition for supremacy over the planet in the old world. The old world developed on the lines of a war machine capable of mass destruction of its own species.

Nevertheless, these separations, both physical barriers and biological differences could not separate the humans into such diverse forms that they could not cross all physical barriers and biological differences to unite as one society. A society capable of assuming a form that is a mixture of all the different human races. That has characteristics of all human races. That the entire humanity has a central form, a combination of all human races fused together. The humans could produce a union of all colours and hues in which all-biological differences and political thinking could merge as one and bring harmony on the planet.

However, human history is one of division, of despair and hopelessness in the practice of unison of all the human cultures. However, these differences could not create such vast differences in humans to be the cause of hatred and be a reason for invasions and wars.

MARCH OUT OF EUROPE AND THE FIRST CITIES

Around 6500 or 5000 BC, a great impetus in human society took place, although impossible to prove or quite difficult to assess. However, during this time, there could have been a population explosion in the European Continent. The tribes in Northern most extremities might have effected a ripple effect throughout Europe and later on in the Mediterranean and finally into the Middle East and South Asia.

It seems that the civilizations that sprang on the Mediterranean Coasts and the river valleys of the Nile, the Tigris, and Euphrates and the culture that arose in the Indus valley seem in part all connected. These civilizations seem created by the same people. These civilizations seem created due to this ripple effect in Europe and by the people who were responsible for this ripple effect. The temperature of Europe, after 10, 000 BC, started becoming temperate from tundra type climate. With this, there was bound to be an increase in population as this environment was conducive for the support of sufficient flora and fauna, which in turn could support a large human population.

As the tribes in the Northern parts became to swell in numbers, it was out of their need that they took to the sea. To take to the sea they might have thought a lot about inventing transportation that could take them long distances across the water bodies that blocked their progress into other parts of the planet. Although other human races have also invented the boat to suit their local environments and needs. Nevertheless, history has proven that the European human has excelled in exploration. The explorers from Europe have shone on the land, the sea, and the interstellar space. The voyages undertaken by the European races on the high seas, the unchartered lands explored by the European explorers and geographers and the stars measured by the European astronauts and cosmonauts are at present, unparalleled in the history of the world. This race due to some selective pressure has gained an advantage at this particular trait over the other races.

In addition, if we go by the historical records as witnesses and infer from these records. A conclusion drawn from this that the first boats invented to cross the barriers of human segregation came up in dockyards of Europe. These boats built on Europe's Northern and Western coasts by the sailors who had desire to go beyond ordinary human scope.

Due to interactions among humans of Europe, their technology dissipated among the cultures that flourished on that continent. Nevertheless, it could have been but a matter of time, when the Northern tribes either by sword or otherwise put migratory pressure on their cousins down South. It could have been possible that the tribes from Northern Europe like their descendants centuries later, The Vikings, took long voyages themselves, made their ways first to different continents. Then through inter connected water bodies to establish civilizations on different corners of these inter connections. Because during those times the world geography and topography was very different from what it is now. Where there is land initially, it could have been water or a large lake in those times.

When these "Sea People" established colonies at these places on the African- Asian land mass, others might have followed. On the other hand, even a continuous communication with their original homeland might have continued. In time, such colonies would have grown, developed, and turned into magnificent centres of trades and eventually into large cities. For all the river valley civilizations and the Mediterranean Civilizations that sprang during the start of the Bronze Age, sprang up almost simultaneously.

These large cities built with great planning, labour, and toil might have taken many years. The toil generated by the beasts of burden that the European immigrants could find in the tropical lands they had come to inhabit. Human endeavour exercised by the enslaved labour that the people from the Northern hemisphere might have captured from neighbouring localities and used them for building monuments too contributed in building these cities. Maybe they could not build such centres of civilizations in their European homelands. They could not find enough slave labour to build for them in Europe and because among their own people these seafarers were not at any particular advantage to enforce such terms. They found the local North African-Asian populations primitive and disorganised. Hence easy to enslave and rule. It was the same during colonial periods of 1800 AD and 1900 AD, when the European countries had taken over almost the entire world. Until the European powers' mutual jealousy and distrust brought havoc and destruction upon each other and ended Europe's ascendancy upon the world.

The people from Europe did not penetrate into the lands inhabited by the Mongloid People, neither the Negroid People. Hence, these types of river valley civilization remains are until present times not found in these geographical locations. Hence, it is safe to write that the Pre dynastic Nile Valley Civilizations, Euphrates-Tigris Valley Civilizations, Elam, Civilizations in Anatolia and the around the Mediterranean were built by the sea faring people from Europe. These civilizations built up through a long time of development. These civilizations sprang up favoured by change in environment that was warmer and moist from the original homeland of these 'seafarers'. Moreover, this environment invigorated these people into developing a civilization with new features beyond human capability of the times. They could never build such cities in their cold barren homelands.

Seeing the planning and systematics of these cities and close similarities between their architecture there can be no doubt that, the people who were responsible for these civilizations somehow related to each other, maybe ethnically. That these people were not of indigenous population is obvious. The magnitude and insight of town planning and the civic administration required to maintain such centres of human activity are, even at present times, quite difficult to maintain by the indigenous populations in the African-Asian countries. No Eastern nation either under self-ruled democratic, autocratic, or dictatorial form of governments has built anything like these cities. Hence, the people who built these cities were not from the indigenous population.

The idea of Kingship in the Middle Eastern and South Asian societies of the ancient past have always depicted the Monarchs as celestial beings or having a divine presence among the subjects. Priest Kings and 'Son of the Gods' had much prevalence in the ancient kingdoms. These titles prefixed before the names of monarchs signified that they were not among the people. That these rulers were not indigenous and were in fact sea faring people from Europe who had set up these kingdoms and referred to as divine beings by the local enslaved populations. It was just like the arrival of the Conquistadors in the New World and seen as Gods by the Native American people. Due to their fair colours and varied eye pigments, they were very different from the population of South America. Their large boats, which the natives had never seen nor they could build, too fascinated the natives. It is possible that the Natives considered the seafarers as Gods, coming out of deep oceans during ancient times.

The ritualistic prostrations performed in the presence of a monarch in the cultures of the Middle East and South Asia too points towards this. It meant as if the monarch was a being of heavenly descent. This practise was also the remnant of old times. Later this practise carried further down the ages. Moreover, it deeply engraved in the Eastern populations during the times old and new. In Europe, these prostrations were unknown, as among their own kind no one was above the other and neither any one was visually different to receive any special attention and admiration.

It is visible, that after these civilizations ceased to exist the local populations or kingdoms that arose one after the other. Century after century on the ruins of one another have not been able to replicate or duplicate these River Valley Civilizations. Such level of sophisticated civic planning and town structure with broad lanes, and near effective town planning with logistic support to cater to the population was present in Rome. However, Rome was in Europe.

Even in those continents where the European powers had set up colonial states in the early modern age, once the Europeans left after the World War II to restructure and repair their own countries. That been destroyed by the war that raged in Europe. The well-planned and structured cities that they built in their colonies were left to decay and rot under the self-governance of the local populations. In almost all such cities, that the European rulers have built during the colonial period, heaps of garbage and large masses of shantytowns are scattered around the cities. These urban sites have little or no sanitation control. Nor any logistic planning carried out by the local authorities to cater to the need of the populations that dwell in such cities.

Anyhow, during the times of the early valley civilizations, after a long time of flourishing there might have been geographical changes. Along with political and anthropological changes as well. The population that arrived from Europe lived and interacted with the local population for many years. Later, due to changes in the climate and cut off from their original homeland after the seas dried up, they slowly mingled with the local population. Albeit with much reluctance and resistance against inter breeding, due to differences in racial features and behaviours.

This racial mingling made them lose their distinct identity and with slow dilution in their blood, their genetic structure that made them plan and execute on organised lines faded away. With time, as this happened, their cities fell in decay. Finally, these civilisations vanished. Some destroyed by war and taken over by invaders like in the Nile Valley, The Tigris-Euphrates Valley, and Anatolian Cities. Some cities were lost in time without a trace. Leaving no records, as to what mystery ended their existence until recovered by removal of dust that had gathered upon their ruins by the turmoil of time. Like some cities in the Mediterranean and the Indus Valley that were discovered by chance.

The cities that were further down South were lost first and those up North in the Middle East were not lost that easy. In some places like the in the Nile Valley or The Tigris-Euphrates Valley it was mere change of rulers. In these places, there was constant influx of migration from the Northern Hemisphere. In addition, infusion of blood of the original people who built these cities remained coming in from the pool in which it spawned.

Then there were invasions from the other European tribes from the Europe lands that bordered with Central Asia. The tribes that moved from Eurasia (Europe-Central Asian Steppes) into the Middle East, crossing the shallow water bodies that prevented such migrations in the past, also mingled with the local populations. Moreover, were instrumental in bringing down these early river valley civilizations and building their own civilizations on the ruins of the older civilizations.

Whatever the reason for the coming up of these civilizations their cause was human invention to overcome natural barriers and expand into the world. As evolution had given, some human races the gift of invention that proved to be their edge over other races. When these cities flourished the written word was very different from the words that the later civilizations communicated in. this makes these civilizations a bit different from the civilizations that are our direct progenitors.

The written word used by these early river valley civilizations used pictures to depict spoken words. Strangely, it is common to all these early world civilizations. This is a proof to strengthen the argument that the people who laid the foundations of these far-flung civilizations related to each other in some way. Because their cultures resembled each other architecturally, alphabetically and possibly racially means that these civilizations were creations of the same people.

By 2000 BC OR 1800 BC probably, the shallow water bodies that segregated the humans in Africa mainland from North Africa were finally giving way. Europe from Middle East and Europe and Middle East from China Mainland and Eastern part of Asia had dried out. These shallow lakes might have filled with sediments that flowed into them. Finally, there was no water left in these lakes. They dried up just like the drying up of the Caspian Sea in the modern times.

With the turn of events, human migration also took another turn because with the water drying up in these lakes. It also changed the climatic conditions of the planet and throw up new challenges for the primate called the human. Moreover, these events forced humans to migrate up and down the planet through new land routes.

Land Connections and Drying up of the Seas of Separation

Around 4000 BC or 3500 BC, these early river valley civilizations were definitely nearing their end. Since the shallow seas had dried up. This brought climatic changes around the planet in form of newly formed deserts and steppes. Moreover, new routes of migration opened up.

This also meant that the isolated European population, which was responsible for the River Valley Civilizations, cut off from its distant homeland from where it was receiving fresh immigrants to populate its armies, constabularies, and bureaucracy. While the workers still were from the local dark skinned populations. Generations of these European people grew up and died in these large metropolitan cities. While new people constantly arrived through the sea route to reinforce their population, so at first their culture did not change much. This culture was going through new experiences. Exposure to such growing experiences in Europe was impossible. These new and varied influxes had an invigorating effect on the culture of these people just as it is happening in the North American Continent.

However, with the sea routes dried up, the cities flourished at the mercy of the rivers for maritime journeys to the high seas. Moreover, it was an arduous journey to reach these cities while by passing whole continents if to reach these places from Europe. Hence, the new immigration stopped altogether from the destinations that were located in the Northern hemisphere. The people living in these cities, with each passing generation lost touch with their past, after these cities got land locked. It brought about inter breeding with the local population, as is the law of nature. After many centuries of forgotten past, the populations of these cities became indigenous. In addition, so did their thinking pattern and social behaviour, which was markedly different from the founders of these civilizations.

As time went by the climate of Northern hemisphere mellowed down and became more temperate for human survival. Under such conditions, human population started swelling and was ready for making inroads down South. However, this time the marine barriers were not there to stop them from coming into North Africa and Asia. This period gives us a good record of the historical events that were taking place at that time. For the alphabets of this time are quite understandable. It is from this period that we derive our alphabets. Therefore, we can discern what our ancestors were writing in their records. Moreover, what they meant to convey through their written words.

The written word that developed during this time used the alphabet with little use of the pictures. It is easy to infer that the alphabet was a special code in which to communicate. In addition, it was the privilege of a few and a closely guarded secret. The people who kept the secret of this code were the priestly classes. In addition, they did not want to make their knowledge public. Hence, everyone could become 'knowledgeable'.

The later Nile Valley Civilizations called the Dynastic Period of the Pharaohs during this time speak of a 'Sea People' making raids on the lands of the Pharaohs. Moreover, from the pictures of that time the 'Sea People' have a remarkable resemblance to Greek Hoplites. It means that the Sea People were no doubt immigrants from Europe making inroads into North African territories.

While some European people were exerting population pressures on the North African Kingdoms. The others were marching into Asia through North Western Asia and Central Asian Routes that bordered on the East of Europe. These people came into Asia along with their war beasts. This pulled their chariots and mounted the warriors on their backs, the horse. The European people had domesticated and bred the horse when they reached Southern Russian Steppes. Moreover, it was instrumental in their victories over the Asian Racial Groups. Except the Mongloid people, who themselves were masters in equine breeding. Knowledge they most probably acquired from the Aryan immigrants.

The period from 4000 BC TO 2000 BC is a period of constant migration. Wave after wave of tribes moved from the North of Europe to its South, with its ripple effect into the Middle East and Central Asia. This effect at times created new kingdoms, destroyed, and ruined by a new wave of invaders from the North. Who themselves were displaced from their homes by some fierce tribe migrating from further North. Now that we can fairly understand the human population dynamics of the time, we can take one continent at a time during this period and those that followed.

Europe during this time was changing. Its changing climate was responsible for its changing demography. The Northernmost parts, the Scandinavia was very much like it is today, may be a bit cold, with temperate summers and cold winters. However, place was sending the waves of immigrations throughout the world. The climate during this time was pleasant than it was before. Hence, there was general rise in human population. This spread towards Central, Eastern, Western, and Southern Parts of Europe, both by sea and by land through the woodlands that divided the Scandinavian lands from Central Europe. However, these adventures of the Northman displaced the people who had come from the North just like them and settled in the warmer parts centuries ago. These people pushed into Asia Minor, Central Asia, and North Africa.

In North Africa, they were the 'Sea People' in most probability. While the Hittites who conquered Asia Minor was also from this stock. So were the Assyrians. Because the Hittites and the Assyrians both used horse drawn chariots. This, the chariot was weapon unknown in Asia, before the rise these two cultures. The horse drawn chariots of the Hittites and the Assyrians instilled fear in the Asian armies. When the Asian armies faced them on battlefield, the Asian tactics were obsolete. In many such encounters, these newly arrived immigrants decimated the Eastern armies with much savagery and bloodshed. Such war was unknown to the Eastern armies on the battlefield.

In Asia during this time, the previous civilizations had mingled with the local populations and there was much change in racial mix of the population. This change also brought about change of rulers. As new empires built upon the old, Babylon and other empires like it, which were a mixture of the old alien culture and the indigenous cultures sprang up. However, had existed with continuity, replaced the old Sumer. The new empires did have knowledge of the past civilizations that they had replaced. Moreover, they had huge racial element of these past civilizations in the existent population. Although Babylon too was a great civilization but the older Sumer was much more organised and gave the world much more than Babylon. All the irrigation system, the record keeping, farm taxation and governance practices that Babylon adopted were remnants of Sumerian culture. Babylon did not possess the free spirit of Sumer neither in practice nor in soul. Hence, it lacked the vigour, just like the Modern Middle Eastern Countries, caught between progress and tradition.

The Indus Valley Civilization after its surrounding seas dried up, existed for some time, without vitality. The population slowly lost its past identity, as it had no contact or communication with its homeland. This population might have been indifferent to change. The mixture of these European people with local population might have been very little, if it did occur. The urban life of Indus Valley Cities during these times would have been uneventful, barren with loss of creativity. With every passing year and collection of silt took these cities farther away from the ocean so did their European spirit.

In North Africa during this period, the Pharaohs who were a mix of the people from Europe and the old inhabitants replaced the Pre Dynastic Period. They too created a culture that was a mix of the people from the North and the Indigenous people. In addition, was very different from the system of the old civilization, without impetus, without force, without energy. Under the Pharaohs, oppression and absolute authority was rule of the day just it is in the present North Africa. It was a glorified police state with a divine dictator at its head.

The arrival of immigrants from Europe meant war for these civilizations. These civilizations carried out their daily existence with farmers toiling to fill the granaries of the ruling class, and exploited by the traders. The traders in turn were under the iron thumb of the officials of the throne. While the aristocracy including the nobility indulged in hunting and vagaries of every possible way and none worried about governance. The political conditions were much like the governments of the third world countries effete, and decadent.

The arrival of tribes from the North who believed in equality among peers, tribal loyalty infused very deeply among the clans and a life of free spirit, were more than a match, for the armies of the North African and Asian Rulers. Thankfully, for the Middle East, the invaders were not much in numbers. In addition, they settled in Asia Minor, the Mediterranean part of Asia (Lebanon, Syria, Palestine etc. . .), Upper Part of the Persian Plateau. Moreover, could not make many inroads deeper into both the continents because the strength in numbers did not favour these people. These people founded new kingdoms in these parts and changed the racial feature of the people of this region. They turned the people much fairer then the rest of the inhabitants of Asia. Even until this day, the people of this region have habits, which are distinguishably European than Asian.

As the sea had dried up, some of the European people made inroads into the newly created land on the Central Asian Steppes. Moreover, spread far off until they reached the borders of the Gobi Desert and outskirts of Mongolia and led a nomadic life style. These people had the horse as a central figure in their life. In addition, it is a certainty that these tribes reached Eastern extremities of Central Asia. These people mixed with the Mongoloid People. This inbreeding infused new blood into the Mongoloid people. Most probably, these Caucasian tribes were the ones who took the horse and the compound bow into the Altai Region. Because the Aryan expansion during this time, especially on horseback and horse drawn chariots all point that the Aryans were most probably the ones who introduced the horse in Central Asia.

It is also possible that this interbreeding was the cause of the origin of the Chinese Civilization. When these Aryan People mixed with the Mongloid People, this mixture brought new ideas that mixed with the ideas of the Mongoloid people. It created a civilization that was unique only to the China. In addition, its elements passed on to South East Asian Cultures through dissemination of trade and commerce. Along with immigration and conquest, it spread into all of Far East.

It was during the spread of the Aryan culture into North African sands, into Asian fields and steppes that the seeds of Chinese Culture sowed. Towns and cities on the riverbanks had come up later in time in the Chinese lands. This civilization raised much later then the river valley civilizations of the Middle East and the South Asian Sub-continent. When the Aryans spread out of Europe, first

Chinese River Valleys sprang up. The push that the Chinese civilization received at this time could most possibly be due to the interaction between the European Immigrants and the Mongoloid Settlers, in the China Mainland. This new Chinese culture also spread down into the Southern regions of South East Asia. As made out from similarity in all Mongoloid Cultures, in their sculptures, writings, and languages.

Human past has proven that, though, European people have a long history of coming out of their continent to disperse into other lands, occupied by other human races. The other races have shown no such inclinations and have not tried to immigrate into the European lands during historical times. Hence, all innovations that Europe could provide to the world were through these immigrations and invasions. In return, the Eastern people of settled life could not provide much for the European world. Even if they did, it was miniscule compared to what it received from the Europeans in the past or the present.

ARYAN INVASIONS

2000 BC to 1500 BC was a period of another expansion out of Europe of the 'Fair Skinned, Horse Riding Warriors. This period saw the end of the Hittites and the Assyrians and the ascendancy of the Persian-speaking people or the Aryans on the Iranian Plateau.

This period again saw an outburst of human migration into the Asia. However, this time it was through the South Eastern Europe and North Western Central Asia. It too was most probably the outcome of a push from the Scandinavia into interior Europe. This spread into the Asian heartland. These migrations laid the foundations of the Latin Civilizations, both the Greek and Roman. Due to the consequences of this great wave the Indo European 'Aryans' spread onto the North Western Asia, Iran, The Central Asian Plateau far off till Mongolia. Moreover, they spread until the outer reaches of the Chinese Civilization. It could be possible they these people penetrated into the Mongoloid dominated Trans Ural Regions too. However, these migrations for the time, made the Indo European culture the pre dominant culture in the Western part of the Middle East and nearly all of Central Asia.

When these people emerged from the Northern Parts of Europe into the Southern Parts, they displaced many tribes in their way. They took over the already established people, who too came from the North centuries ago. These earlier people settled in these regions very much the same way. These two peoples intermingled, so did their culture to form the Latin Culture. This culture later made world famous by the Greeks and the Romans. This culture laid much emphasis on scientific thought, republican government, and bodily vitality. For the protection of their civilization, they depended on a well-oiled military machine. Theirs was perhaps the first military to develop procedures in which collective strength of common soldiers were employed to form complicated battle formations. Such battle formations showed the discipline infused in these cultures even during ancient times.

These people also spread into the Spain and the Coastal North Africa, albeit slowly. They replaced the Iberian population that dug in there before these people. These Iberian People could have been the progenitors of the Phoenicians. Who had founded maritime colonies in the Mediterranean and the North Africa, after displaced from Europe. The new comers in Spain and the Mediterranean were free spirited people and believed in individual freedom. The monarch was not an absolute person but a part of their society who wielded power through the trust of his people, by setting some personal examples.

These same people first settled in the Balkans and finally entered the Asia Minor through the mountain passes and found an already established Hittite kingdom. The Hittite culture formed because of the same reasons of population displacement. They had arrived in these lands from Europe through the same passages. The Hittites settled in this region just like these new invaders had entered this territory. These new invading people took over the Hittites or at least were instrumental in their decline. However, the new comers' immigration wave was diverted eastwards by the Hittites who could survive a little longer.

At the same time, another branch of these invading people entered Asia through the Russian Steppes and spread towards the East. Most probably, they became founders of the Scythians and the Tocharas, the Persians too were part of this line. While the Scythians and the Tocharas spread out in the Steppes of Central Asia. The Persians entered the Iranian Plateau, destroyed the Assyrians, and slowly seeped their culture into the Iranian Plateau. Until these people overwhelmed the remnants of Babylon. The Scythians and the Tocharas spread into Southern part of Central Asia as well and occupied the highlands of Modern Afghanistan as far as Tibet.

The Indus Valley Culture influenced the Indian Sub Continent's North Western part, during this time. The Persians who had reached until the mountains of Baluchistan had been in contact with these people. To the Persians these people were 'Hindus' a word derived from 'Sindhus', inhabitants of Hind or 'Sind'. No doubt, they were descendants of the same people who had created the Indus Valley Civilization. Even until this day the people of India, the Hindus, worship the deities that are 'Non Aryan. The practice of the worship of Mother Goddesses is itself a practice carried in all River Valley Civilizations of the past. A practice carried out from the times of Indus Valley Civilization. This particular civilization was not at good terms with the Persian Empire. This understood from literature of the ancient Persian texts.

It was but a matter of time when the Aryans who had settled in Southern Central Asia, ventured into the Indian Sub-Continent and were in conflict with the already established society of the region. The invading 'Aryans' described the local population living in castles and walled cities. Moreover, they worshiped strange deities and the 'phalluses, a practice still taking place in India. These Aryan invaders were instrumental in spreading the Hindu civilization into the interior of the Indian Sub-Continent from the North Western part of India. They were responsible for spreading it into the Proto Austroloid dominated Gangetic Plains and the Central Indian Plateau. Their invasions made the 'Hindus' penetrate deeper into the Indian Subcontinent and displace or mix with the Austroloid population. The North Western parts of the Indian Sub-Continent became Aryan or 'Vedic. The Eastern parts became Brahminical, the descendants of the remnants of the Indus Valley civilizations, retaining their form of worship and social practices. The 'Aryan' texts speak of their Gods destroying the stone castles of their enemies and driving the enemies' armies into the oblivion.

Thus at the end of this period, these people who can now be termed as Indo Europeans had spread into the Northern Western Asia, the Iranian Plateau, The Central Asia, North Western India, and the coasts of North Africa. Thus, the Indo Europeans meant European people who had spread out from Europe and spread until India along with the culture of Europe and their languages. Even until date, these languages share many common features among the Indo European people despite centuries of separation.

The contact of these people with the Mongloid people of the East could have been responsible for vitalizing the Mongoloid people into establishing a civilization of its own. These people were responsible for establishing cities in the China Mainland along the river valleys. Contact with Africa mainland was much restricted due to logistical setbacks. In addition, whatever interactions that there were, did not account for any cultural infusion.

At the end of this time, that is around 1000 BC, the push of migration from Europe had ceased to be a world-changing event. As there were, no major mass scale population shifts from Europe into other continents after this time for a long time. The reasons for this were the at the population of major parts in the Middle East and North Africa ruled by the immigrating European tribes stopped the invasions from Europe into these areas due to somewhat matched military strength and similarity in culture. This advantage remained until the Indo Europeans slowly lost their European identity through the elements of environment and dilution of their European blood with the local population.

Struggle for the Middle East

Around 500 BC until 500 AD there had been a long struggle in the Middle East. Europe tried to establish its hegemony inside the Asian and North African territories. The European tribes and people had much success over the North Africans and Asians of the Middle East and Central Asia.

From 500 BC until 300 AD, Europe was a place ripe with ideas. Ideas of freethinking and philosophical enterprise that took place nowhere else in the world were flowing in Europe. These ideas were prevalent especially in the South Western Europe and the Southern Parts of this continent. At the beginning of this time, the Greek culture led the way. It was full of vigour and strength, and its culture was expanding on the ideas of its philosophers. European culture grew in leaps and bounds in scientific thought, political ideas and military might, during this time.

The new ideas of governance had taken the European tribes out of the context of a tribe into a republican system in the Mediterranean. It was one of the greatest ingenuity invented by man for the progress of society. This thought was very indigenous to Europe. Other societies of that time could not come up with such a form of government. Why other societies did not think it up, is indeed a matter of concern. Why other societies remained indifferent to the idea of republicanism? Why they remained slaves to the system of monarchy? It is indeed curious. A republic created and practised by the Southern or the Mediterranean People of Europe, especially in the Mediterranean took these people above the tribal setup. A republic was a city, in which large numbers of people were citizens. Moreover, they found a way to exist and carry out social activities through popular consent. Maybe it was the cause of greatness of these civilizations. These small principalities achieved the greatness that large empires of the ancient times could not achieve.

The Greek and Roman civilizations were a Northern European People superimposed upon a culture that too had come from the North a long time ago. This new Latin culture had adopted much from the cultures of North African Kingdoms and that of the Asian Civilizations before and during the periods of the republics. Hence caught between the Barbarian and bellicose tribes of the North and large lines of battle formations of empires of the South these 'Latin' people developed military tactics that suited both adversaries. The government that they invented was a tribal political system revised for city life.

These people developed a republican thought. It was a mixture of the tribal society of the North and the administrative necessities of vast empires of the South. It was a perfect balance of the two. This system also promoted common good and spirit of cohesion between the people, who were citizens of these republics. It was just like the concept of patriotism of later times in Europe.

Under such a system, people grew in science, commerce, and enterprise because their republics were not repressive for the citizens. The people of these Republics were repressive towards the slaves though. These were the first societies that recognised the value and advantage of an ordered living. They knew the importance of discipline in making progress in all facets of cultural improvement.

No doubt, the freedom of thought and speech gave the philosophers enough space to question the natural world and observe the way it behaved. It infused a spirit of adventure and free will in the youth of that time. People indulged in dialogues to solve the mysteries of nature and the world that surrounded these people. It was only because of such a system that first the Greek and then the Roman Cultures could make inroads into the North African and Asian domains through conquest.

The North African and Asian Cultures were repressive and against the culture of free spirit. These cultures were stagnant and lifeless. The Eastern kingdoms were bound to the ideals of servility of the masses towards the nobility and the ruling class. In these societies, the ruling classes were oppressors and the subject classes lived on a different plane altogether, with no spirit to fight or to stand up and speak out. The European armies that marched into the realms of the Eastern Empires were patriotic armies, joined in a common cause and common good. Their armies trained in a manner that infused much discipline and unity among the soldiers. These tactics were only possible because of the idea of a republican way of life.

When faced with European armies the vast cohorts of Asian or North African Armies, although much superior in numbers lacked the discipline to stand ground against a disciplined and a well drilled enemy. An army that recognised the importance of coordinated action and coherence was definitely at an advantage. That learnt from experience and thoughts of the philosophers who studied military tactics in a scientific method could easily rout such an enemy. The Eastern Armies could never understand or conceptualize these ideas of discipline. It was not in their culture to grow on collective strength of numbers. In addition, they depended on individual growth and personal betterment rather than overall benefits for their people. The Western armies developed battle formations in which every single man was an important pillar. This was reason that Alexander and the descendants of many of his Generals and later the Romans captured and held Middle Eastern Lands under them for great lengths of time with great ease. These European rulers provided stability to these lands that the previous rulers of local descent could not provide.

When Alexander marched into the Eastern World, even during those days, the Eastern World was not that advanced as the European Republics were. While the European World, especially the Mediterranean was in an orderly state there was much disorganisation and indiscipline in the Eastern World. This disorder and indiscipline was evident even during the battles between the Macedonian Greek combined armies and the armies of the Eastern kingdoms and empires. It was typically a battle between order and disorder.

The ancient European King, even Phillips and Alexander, were treated like Chiefs of a clan. They were not some pompous Eastern King imprisoned in his courtroom and distant from the people. Neither did the people of Europe tolerate oppressive tyrants and wanted their leader to lead in every sphere of life, be it battle or civility. Nevertheless, even Alexander, The Great, could not resist the corruption offered to him in the Eastern court. Although he was a man of vision and very well educated for his times that too under the great philosophers like Aristotle himself. Who was very much aware of the Eastern corruption in political theory and had discussed much of its faults with his pupils.

Under the Greeks and later the Romans, the lands of Middle East and Asia that were under their control did definitely prosper. As they had not done before the rule of these new rulers controlled these lands. The Roman armies due to their military tactics were able to move into the Northern parts of Europe itself. This was a complete reverse of what was happening for centuries. The invasions came from the North and not from the South before this time. This reversal came to be possible due to fusion between the Eastern and the Western military practices. In addition, the military tactics that this fusion bred proved successful in Europe itself.

It was also during this time that the Siberian lands too had an explosion of population and it was moving from the East to the West for the first time. During this time, the Mongloid tribes increased in numbers in Altai regions. Moreover, their great numbers made inroads into the Caucasian held Central Asia. Nevertheless, these tribes did have a lot of Caucasian blood flowing in their veins. This had changed these people a lot and had taught these nomads to make effective use of the horse. Europeans domesticated the horse in European lands. Moreover, they introduced it into the Eastern parts through nomadic tribes that ventured out of Europe and reached the Altai regions. They most probably ventured deep into Chinese lands, albeit not in large numbers to change the demography of China Mainland or even Eastern Central Asia. However, definitely they infused their blood within the Chinese bloodlines along with their ideas among the Mongoloid population. For this purpose, the Caucasian numbers were sufficient.

Many Caucasian tribes fled before these Mongloid tribes, while others mixed with them and became the progenitors of the Huns, Turks, and The Tartars. These nomadic Mongloid tribes armed with a potent weapon of that time. The compound bow first fell upon the Chinese Empires but finding them well entrenched and in healthy condition, these migrations turned towards the west.

In the later parts of this period, when these migrations were taking place, west was a place in turmoil. The nomadic people could easily enforce themselves, for the time, on the people of the West. They added to their racial element into the Caucasian people, mostly in the Eastern European and Lower Balkans and Russian territories. These people also pushed many Caucasian nomadic tribes into Anatolia, Persia, Afghanistan, and India.

China Mainland also had great increase of numbers during these periods and greatly enlarged the influence of their culture. Not only did they carve out large empires. They excelled in sciences, arts, and many of the great inventions of the time invented by the Chinese civilizations.

Europe, North Africa, and Asia did not make cultural contact with the people of Interior Africa even at this time. Except that these people started flowing in as slaves from the African countries, carried out by Middle Eastern slave Traders.

During this time, the point of mixture between the cultures of Europe, North Africa and Asia existed where they overlapped each other. These points lay on the lands of the Middle East and provided in the mixing of populations along with ideas. It was for the first time during these times that the Mongloid tribes started penetrating into Central Asia and Europe and on the World Stage.

It is felt that during this time the nomad with his fast moving horse and his compound bow was at an advantage over his sedentary cousin in the other armies. The cultural ideas that were first spreading from the North to the South were now spreading from South and to North and from east to west, as well.

North African and Asian ideas of the Sovereignty of the crown had also started seeping into the European Culture. These ideas started to corrupt the republican system and the spirit of free will and freethinking in the European Lands. The coming of these ideas into the European Lands also led to and started to push the civilizations, which had previously excelled in many good things in the field of governance, into the abyss of decay. In this confusion, the nomad with his free spirit and unrepressed thinking and love of adventure was at an edge over his European counterparts. In addition, that made him superior on the battlefield, when he entered in hordes into Europe.

This period was responsible for decay of the European Civilization because many evils of the North African and Asian ideas on kingship had penetrated into the psyche of the rulers of Europe. Instead of evolving Europe had devolved. These were the reasons responsible for the downfall of the Romans. Once they were a people known for their honest labour and discipline. During the times when Rome was a republic, it was very different from the days of the Emperors. During this period, their Emperors were famous for debauchery because they enjoyed unprecedented powers. Their society was intolerant towards freethinking. They adopted these ideas from their North African and Asian Territories that the Romans had conquered.

Scientific thinking and progress completely halted in a repressive Europe during this time and a period of Dark Age set in. This culture was foreign to the Europeans. It spread among its ruling class with the immigration of many Asian people in large numbers into European cities and countryside. These ideas infected the nobility and the landowners easily, because these ideas gave them great powers over their subjects.

During these times, invaders were coming into Europe from all sides due to its political policies that had weakened the continent. From the South, the Persians were knocking at its gates while the nomadic peoples who at first were Caucasians, were penetrating the Eastern borders of Europe. Later on, many mongoloid tribes too entered Europe and made it their home. It shows the vulnerability of Europe once it adopted Eastern type of governance.

The coming of these new people from the Asian lands could have been one of the reasons that democracy and republican character of European cities and kingdoms could not flourish for a long time. It was responsible for taking Europe into the dark ages. As the people who had immigrated from the East, infected by monarchical ideas of their homelands spread it among the European people. Europe too became much Eastern. Since these new people ruled in many parts of Europe by the sword, they were responsible for destruction of democratic principles in Europe. The stage for authoritarian regimes in Europe that eventually took Europe down into the Dark Ages was the creation of this setting.

This period saw a struggle between the Roman Civilization and the Zoroastrian Civilization and a clash of ideas, which slowly intertwined into each other. The Persian Empire, whose state religion was Zoroastrian, advocated its spread through means at the disposal of the state and persecuted other religious beliefs. It provided absolute authority to the Emperor, and his Governors through the High Priests. Much like the clergy of the medieval Europe provided authority to the Holy Roman Emperors. However, the Zoroastrian idea of absolute authority of the state and its doctrine of suppression of any thought that deviates from the popular belief, slowly crawled into Roman thought and politics.

When the Roman Civilization adopted Christianity, it adopted the teachings of the Christ along with many Doctrines of Zoroastrian Priestly class. Doctrines regarding heresy and persecutions were all very Persian. The teachings of Christ were for the masses as he himself was a person of humble origins. He advocated that masses indulge in honest labour and not indulge in corrupt methods and in means of exploitation. Christianity never advocated persecution neither it was in the culture of the Jews as Christ was one of them. Christianity has much in common with Judaism. In fact, the people of Christ for centuries themselves had become the targets of persecution. Since Zoroastrianism was a state religion and its priestly class enjoyed protection of the state, the church adopted the policy of persecution as recognised by Sassanid's state religion. It is evident from many historical records that during the period of Zoroastrianism in Persia no other religion propagated within in the Persian Empire under a well-formulated state policy. Especially during the latter parts of Achaemenid Dynasty and during the entire period of the Sassanid Dynasty, no one could propagate theories that were not part of the Zend Avesta.

The Church became an effective tool of suppression even in matters that were in the realm of science and philosophy and did not even remotely touch on politics. However, such behaviour of the authorities ultimately led to the downfall of the Roman Empire.

It was a period never witnessed in European history. The innovative thoughts that the Christian Church tried very hard to destroy including the progressive thinking in the philosophical mind of the European philosophers, made Europe ignorant. All science that Europe discovered and practised based upon the thinking and open discussions of the philosophers were lost. Not only science but sociology too built on the foundations of the thoughts of the philosophers. However, philosophical thought diminished in Europe.

The Church by supressing the freethinking of the philosophers and through its advocacy of repressive methods dulled European ingenuity into a very uninventive silence. This silence took life out of the European society. The life that had made Europe different from other societies of the world was not present there. The life that had made the European armies much more disciplined than other armies was more in disarray than the other parts of the world. The life that made European society more tolerant and progressive and the way it welcomed new ideas. Moreover, innovations had become more intolerant than other social setups of the time.

Roman Empire fell because it fell into an abyss of darkness and ignorance. This darkness prevented scientific thought and spirit of honest labour. The society lacked discipline, the spirit of republicanism, and a spirit of adventure. The tools of the State effectively and thoroughly suppressed all positive values. Political or religious arms, in a vain attempt to protect their own interests crippled the very spirit, which founded Rome. The ruling class of Rome ultimately destroyed those things that made Rome great. Ultimately, they destroyed themselves along with Rome.

Rome was a great power with a disciplined army and a vibrant population progressing with great speed. Rome destroyed itself by a few virulent ideas. These ideas infected it through its Asian and North African Neighbours. It lost its own identity and fell an easy prey to an ill equipped and a barbarian army never to rise from its ashes. The barbarian army that was responsible for the fall of Rome, rather, the entire tribes that followed this army, finally entered the North African lands.

Nevertheless, even this migration of Europeans into North Africa, could not change the way people of North Africa perceived governance and society. In time, these new arrivals too caught up and consumed in the Eastern traditions. In addition, could not create a society that could compete with the land from which these barbarians had come from, to settle on the African Lands.

However, even after Rome reduced to a heap of bricks and mortar the ideas that destroyed it spread to the rest of

Europe and the Eastern Roman Empire. If the historians call this period the 'Dark Ages' in Europe they were wrong. The entire world was living in the dark ages as repression, subjugation was idea of the time, and the ruling class indulged in it. The entire human world carried itself without any care for human progress and advancement, whether in Europe, Africa, or Asia.

During this time, the landowners exploited the serfs and farmers with much brutality to fill the granaries. There was no advancement because religion prevented freethinking and innovative ideas to spread among the general population. It was a common phenomenon among all the cultures of those days especially in the later periods, and the life of the common folk was very difficult and oppressive.

During these periods' cultural exchanges between the Mongloid World and the West including The Middle East were very rare, but on the Steppes of Central Asia a rapidly growing and expanding Mongloid Nomadic population overcame the Caucasian people, who too were nomads, who had occupied these lands long ago. In these territories, there was in fact much mixing between the Caucasian and the Mongloid Nomadic People.

The Semitic and Aryan population of Middle East experienced much interbreeding where these two populations fringed upon each other. This mixing of population produced cultural mixes and made diverse human races unify, whenever contact offered a chance, it also led to new creativity, but this creativity was not used in the sphere of political ingenuity to change the world. This racial and cultural mixing produced changes in people and brought about new ideas into the world that had consequences on a global scale in later periods. This mixing of Caucasian and Semitic people laid the foundation of creativity and scientific ingenuity that the later Arab kingdoms and Caliphates displayed.

PERIOD OF DECAY FOR EUROPE AND FOR THE SETTLED CIVILISATION

500 AD to 1000 AD was a time of absolute decay in Europe as a whole. It was a period of relative progress for the Middle Eastern people. It was so, due to the knowledge of the ancient Greeks and Romans made available to people of the Middle East, through the conquests of the Islamic Armies.

In early parts of this period there was a rapid spread of monotheism, this dissipation of monotheistic ideas spread chiefly from empires that had held influence over the people of North Africa, The Near East, The Iranian Plateau and The North Western Central Asia.

This was a time when Rome and the Byzantines had adopted Christianity and were battling an oppressive and strong neighbour in a Zoroastrian Empire in Persia. These empires were strong and well organised, neither was willing to give in to the other, and most of all the state religion of both was monotheistic. With monotheism coming from the east, there were other notions that spread fast into the European lands, that of divinity of the crown.

The European monarch was never a supreme being; he was a leader who had capabilities to lead the people under his command. He never received the treatment that the

Emperors and Kings of Asia and North Africa received from their subjects. The bowings and prostrations of deference that was a practise for the Eastern monarch showed servility of the people. The European Kings of the early times never had such prostrations performed before them. While the Eastern cultures were servile, the European society was not. The European Monarch of the Ancient times never wielded the power of God. Hence, he was from among the people due to the respect of his abilities and was a leader for the protection of his people. He was accessible to most of his army and openly interacted among the people. The European King of ancient times lived in a society that was open and lively.

Even, Alexander, The Great, never received the same honours by his Macedonian phalanx that he received from the remnants of the Persian Court. In the eyes of the Macedonians, he was a general and a leader. For the Persians he was a God, worshipped, and offered gifts of devotion. Such behaviour unjustly corrupts the soul of a person, no matter how enlightened or reasonable. Moreover, it makes a person much authoritarian. It makes the person receiving such honours believe that his presence among the society is a divine intervention.

This notion of the Holiness of the King, with a 'Holy Roman Emperor, that was incorporated into the European Society, made the Monarch, ruler of the land and protector of the religion, something very foreign to the Old European System and was adopted from the Persian System. The Holiness of the monarch in Europe meant suppression of any opposition as a blasphemy against God. New scientific ideas could not spread as they went against the teachings of Bible and this meant a much-oppressed society, which was very much like the societies outside of Europe, be it in North Africa or Asia.

These ideas had infected Rome and Europe through its Eastern Neighbours. As European societies adopted Eastern religion, so did they adopt Asia's ideas about morality and kingship? Europe took up East's belief of absolute authority. Moreover, its repressive and backward thinking that seemed to corrupt the powerful and consume the spirit of the common folk.

Women had enjoyed much freedom in ancient Europe. However, during these times, just like in Eastern societies, the freedom of women was greatly supressed in Europe. This idea, too, came to Europe from the Eastern neighbours, where the treatment of women was like chattel, unlike in ancient European societies. Some ancient European societies had always treated women as equals as is found in many ancient texts. Even the republics of ancient times were not oppressive towards women. They were educated, and many were great philosophers of those times, a rarity in the Medieval Europe.

Hence, from this period or a little earlier the society in Europe did not differ much from the societies of Asian and North African Lands, oppressed and lacking the power that was present in Ancient Europe. Things that gave Europe advantage over other societies were gone when Eastern Ideas of Kingship swept inside Europe. People bowed before the King and had to act servile in his presence. The monarch owned the people through the authority of religion conferred upon him, through the church itself. 'To go against the

Church' meant going against the laws of God. So all people believed what religion taught them.

The area, which was a cause of disagreement between the 'Byzantines' the Eastern Roman Empire, and the Persian Empires, the Western part of Asia caused the destruction of the Roman Civilization. It was in these parts that Eastern ideas spread into the European people's minds and spread to other parts of Europe. In addition, these ideas were strong enough to change the peoples' minds that were outside the borders of the Roman Empire, the barbarian tribes of Western and Central Europe.

The long struggle between these two empires, the Eastern Roman Empire and the Persian Empire might have caused enough destruction and displacements in the Middle East. Moreover, many people fled into the interior of Arabian Peninsula to save themselves from persecution or from war. When these people settled in the Arabian Peninsula, their ideas spread among the local population. Moreover, these ideas might have fascinated the people of the Arabian Peninsula. The monotheistic Semitic religions and to some extent Zoroastrian doctrines of purity and good deeds, advocated the idea of honest labour and had disregard for the lives of people who exploited other hardworking and simple people.

In those times, the priestly class exploited the people of Arabia for a long time and spread superstitions among them. They oppressed the people through the economic policies. Linking such policies with religion the priestly class who ruled over the small trading towns dotting the Arabian Peninsula led luxurious lives. Hence, Prophet Mohammed found readymade recruits for his new faith. People who realized the exploitation of their people by the priests and their unjust religious practices accepted Islam.

Prophet Mohammed created new a faith that had all that Judaism, Christianity and Zoroastrian religion had to offer and combined this new religion into a powerful force. This new religion even until this date is the simplest form of religion that has ever evolved on this planet. It advocated against all the prevailing evils that had spread through the deserts of Arabia right into the heart of Europe. Best of all, it detested exploitation of people and it advocated equality among men, be it a king or a common peasant.

During those times the rulers in all parts of the world believed that, they had a divine right over their subjects. Hence, it was the duty of the subjects to suffer and toil for the monarchs, sent to rule over them by the heavens. Islam advocated the reverse, infused a spirit of unity among its followers. These people were very simple in thought. Pure in their dealings and were untouched by the evils of the society that prevailed in the cities under control of Persia or Constantinople and the lands ruled by these empires. Because these people were uncorrupted, by all the evils that made man trample others of his kind under his feet, these people were free and strong. They achieved much in such short a time.

When these free willed and pure armies rode against the oppressive armies of Persia or Constantinople, the latter armies could not stand their ground against these fresh warriors. Even the population of the lands under Persian and Constantinople control, provided help to these new people. Who emerged from the deserts of Arabia and swept aside the foundations of empires that had stood the tests of time.

As long as, these armies remained pure, their heads bowed in subservience to God, and the principles taught down by Prophet Mohammed, none could stand in their way. They conquered all they encountered. However, it should be known that all whom that these armies destroyed were nothing more than oppressive regimes, who sucked the blood of their subjects.

In time as Islam spread, its religious leaders became rulers, they had less respect for the principles of Prophet Mohammed and more love for their indulgences, and they too in time became oppressive tyrants. They were no better than the rulers from whom they had liberated the people of the conquered territories. This was a period when there was a constant war between the settled form of life and the nomadic way of existence. Nevertheless, the settled form of life with all its pleasantries always corrupted the hardy nomad conqueror.

Things went on like this, when once more, the population in the Altai region became to swell. In addition, the hordes that roamed these grasslands started to become restless. They started to make inroads into Western Parts of Central Asia and Mainland China. Moreover, although these nomads were able to establish foothold on the outskirts of these regions, they could not change much in the fight between the nomad and the settled man. While in the settled lands, the lives of the common people were at the mercy of the ruling class. Moreover, they lived and died at the whims of the people who sat on the thrones.

The suppression of scientific ideas can be very lethal for a society. During the plague or the Black Death, in Europe, lack of scientific knowledge and the consequences of its suppression became evident. The suppression of scientific experiments proved detrimental. As most of these could come under the suspicion of witchcraft or could challenge the authority of Church. The scientific experiments and knowledge they gave could defy the writings of the Bible or other religious books. Hence, all scientific knowledge, including medicine and physiology suffered greatly. This lack of knowledge could not let the European People and their physicians handle the epidemics effectively.

The Muslim kingdoms of these times had advanced in medical science than any European realm could think of. However, the Arabs were progressive in the sciences due to writings that they had received from the Europeans during their conquests in the Roman lands. The Europeans were ignorant of their own researches and philosophical thinking that made Europe great in the past.

Scourge of God Arrives

Times did change between 1000 AD and 1600 AD for the human population. Although that time was brief due to very sudden changes that erupted on the world scene. Human population during this time faced many 'Scourges of God' in the form of butchers and disease. Because the human civilization had reached its upper limit in the cities that could not no longer support the constant influx of people, especially in Europe, The Middle East, and Mainland China. These were the times of change in human civilization. These times created the greatest conflict between the settled form of civilization and the nomadic way of life. The nomads under Genghis Khan, who proclaimed himself the 'Scourge of God', nearly won this conflict.

In the earlier times, the nomadic invasions on the settled communities were due their displacement by a powerful neighbour. This was intent on taking over the grazing lands of the steppes from the earlier occupants. Hence, the displaced nomadic tribes entered the dominions of the settled kingdoms and wrested control of the lands. Lands captured after armed struggle, displacing the existent tribe. However, these invasions and incursions into settled form of life were due to population pressures. These invasions were not due any pre-planned occupational invasion or annexation of the lands beyond population pressures of the nomadic tribes. Hence, these incursions did not bring about mass slaughters or destruction. However, the invasions of the Mongols under Genghis Khan had all the elements of a large-scale invasion, pre-planned under military expansion and for the purpose of occupation and destruction of the sedentary and settled form of life practised by humans who were not nomadic.

The military operations undertaken by the Mongols, made possible due to the knowledge of the weakened state of the sedentary life centres. The authoritarian monarchy and rulers made the sedentary civilisations weak compared to the nomads. These sedentary kingdoms were incapable of sustaining themselves under pressure. The entire civilized world that lived a settled form of life as farmers, artisans, traders, and rulers stratified one above the other; this was an age devoid of human dignity. The people leading a sedentary life were subject to exploitation and savagery of the rulers. Human life was at its lowest during these times. The policy of 'might is right' was prevalent in much of the settled communities.

Some people were leading the lives of Gods or Demi Gods. They had the luxury of tasting every good thing in life. They even had the power to take all that they wanted and acquire all that they wanted. Because they had, the means to enforce their unjust will on most of the society under their thumb and control. While the rest toiled and bled with no hope and respite, there was no justice for the ordinary. The rulers could displace the people like wild beasts or butchered them like sheep, if they wished. At the same time, they could not leave the lands on which they worked unless it was profiting the nobility. Even if a famine were looming over the land, the serfs would not dare leave the place. Those were the times, much like the dictatorship of today prevalent in many Third World Countries.

Democratic institutions were found nowhere in the civilized centres of the world. These centres were known for their towering buildings, big market places and monumental palaces, but civilized they were not. Within the walls of these centres, not all that was progressive, not all that was advancement ever practised. The word of the monarch was law, no matter how wrong or oppressive. The common folk of any town or city had no say in the governance of their place of birth or living. All that the common folk could do was pray for a better life. If not for themselves, then at least they prayed for a better life for their progeny in some distant future.

Nevertheless, such conditions did not exist everywhere on Earth. If there were sedentary centres of life then there were open grasslands and steppes too. The human spirit and human freedom had not crushed under the weight of authoritarian regimes in the grasslands. If not completely free from the oppression and cruelty of one's own species. The nomadic life was quite free from sedentary restrictions. The nomad of ancient times always lived in a democratic system and the leader of the tribe had to excel in promoting the common good of the entire people. The leader of a nomadic tribe was an elected representative. The chief elected in a democratic manner much like the elections of the political leaders of today. The best man could reach to the level of the chief, in whom the entire tribe reposed their faith. Hence, the tribal society was efficient, free of evil, and morally healthy. The tribal people were hardy and full of vigour. The tribal leader did not collect taxes and hence he was not oppressive. He was the leader of his people, to safeguard the pastoral lands and to protect the tribe with the virtue of his leadership.

On the other hand, all huge empires and large kingdoms of the day were more or less like a society of farmers, artisans, and workers controlled by a group of armed hoodlums. Who could take all that the farmer could harvest, all that the worker could toil for and the artisan could produce and create. The monarchs in the settled kingdoms were usually ignorant brutes surrounded by a ring of sycophants. These monarchs took no military exercises or efficient planning for protection of the kingdoms. They could only arm their soldiers and make them collect taxes.

These monarchs and their courts were also unaware of the changing conditions beyond the confines of their cities and forts. In addition, were unprepared for any well-planned military assault that could come in any form. In these empires and kingdoms, the people were under iron control of the rulers. It was a society in which common people were controlled and held ransom by a cruel organisation of nobility, living off the hard work of the people. The armed nobility and their men were predators on the ever-suffering serfs and artisans, devoid of justice and most of all of dignity.

The city dweller had always cheated the simple nomad, whenever the nomad entered the city. The settled communities have looked upon the nomad as a yokel and exploited the nomadic human. Therefore, the nomad too has looked down upon the city dweller with contempt. The nomadic and the sedentary society have always tried to take over one another. Nevertheless, the nomadic life had always provided rulers for the sedentary society. Nevertheless, whenever a nomadic ruler ascended upon the throne of the settled peoples, the nomad was corrupt by the same methods that his predecessors corrupted themselves.

Although no two people are alike, but some people are born to change the world and are seldom corrupted by the niceties that life or wealth has to offer. In addition, such were the people like Genghis Khan and his horde of Mongols.

Genghis Khan spent his younger days as a hostage in a Chinese kingdom. During this time, he observed the inherent weaknesses of the settled kingdoms. The towns, cities, and countryside filled with discontented people who hated their rulers. Genghis Khan himself was of the opinion that the sedentary culture was not the one in which humans should continue. He wanted to destroy all walled cities that enclosed human freedom and within their walls. Within the walls of the cities dignity and honour was not for the ones who toiled and laboured. Whatever the reason that 'Temujin' or Genghis Khan had and whatever methods he employed. All the nomadic tribes 'elected' him their leader. However, most certainly, it was because of his military planning, care of his people and vision that he filled in the tribes. The other nomadic tribes and their leaders admired his qualities and saw hope under his leadership. The election of 'Temujin' as the Great Khan was possible because of a hope that the Tribes had. Otherwise, his election would never have taken place.

Because Genghis Khan knew that, his nomads were more than a match for the soldiers who were under the pay of rulers. So taking one pretext or the other, he entered the dominions of the strong kings and shattered their citadels. Definitely, with the help of discontent populations of the kingdoms he conquered. Such was the hate in his heart for the city life that at times he massacred entire populations and left the cities desolate. His armies destroyed the cities that lay both on the east and on the west of Mongolia.

The Chinese Kingdoms and Empires of the past eras were the only settled form of civilizations, which had effectively repulsed nomadic invasions. Even during the times when the Roman and the Persian Empires could not withstand the onslaught of the nomadic warriors and the sounds of the hoofs of their mounts. The Chinese resisted the nomads effectively. It meant that during the early historical periods, the Chinese civilization was evolving and coming up with new social innovations. The Chinese society was vibrant and a good form of governance practised in these ancient Chinese civilizations. It had excelled in developing effective military techniques for its protection.

Only prosperous and healthy civilizations are capable of acquiring a good military organisation. Moreover, when the nomads invaded Europe or the Persian Plateau, the societies inhabiting these lands were definitely decaying. Hence, they could not face the fresh military tactics of the armies on horsebacks. The Chinese civilization was quite healthy and it was the reason that it could repulse the nomads with great ease. While other great empires of the old days fell before the nomadic warrior.

However, during the invasions of the Mongols under the 'Great Khan', the Chinese people too crumbled very easily. This means that the vibrancy of the Chinese society stopped after these centuries. In addition, the evolution of the Chinese society or civilization came to a halt or slowed considerably.

However, reasons for Genghis Khan's victories were not many, but very simple. A democratic setup of his people and the corruption and degeneration of his enemies were small but at the same times great reasons. The nomad was not a barbarian, as depicted in the stories and tales. Rather, the kings and their armies were barbarians compared to the nomadic warriors. The nomad was a disciplined soldier brought up in a democracy much like that of today. Moreover, rose through the ranks and files because of his individual capacity and not through the rank of his birth.

Whatever damages the Mongols had wrecked upon the large cities, many elements carried it further into many other cities near and far. Disease followed the Mongols trail of destruction. Maybe because of displacement of populations from the Central Asian Kingdoms westwards or from the wide spread death and desolation that the Mongols had spread. The decay of death in Central Asia easily spread into the cities of Middle East, Europe, and China through the caravans and traders. Once inside the cities, unhygienic conditions prevailing during these times helped the infections spread fast and quick. First among the malnourished populations, eventually everyone engulfed in it. However, both these devastations brought the human population down. In addition, at places changed the demography of many geographical locations completely.

The Mongols remained the masters of war as long as their leaders were Khans, as this title symbolized the bearer of the title as leader of a tribe. When the khans became Khagans, which is an imperial title, the Chinese drove them out of the Chinese lands well within a century. Due to the imperial ambitions of these Khagans, their strength and grasp weakened in the Middle East. It was just due to the breakup of the democratic tribal structure that made Mongols raise their heads above other civilizations. However, this imperial change put these nomads on the same platter as other monarchs, authoritarian and corrupt, just as happened before many times.

Nevertheless, in spite of such experiences the human civilization could not change and carried on in the same fashion down the ages from this time. Despite the fact that the form of government practiced during those times was full of frailties. Humans made no effort to rise up against it and put these practices to an end.

It was during these times that the European populations were not able to make any advances into neither the Asian Continent nor the North African lands. Europe held no advantage over its neighbours, in military strategy nor military technology. The conditions of political governance, which during the older times differed between the European and Middle Eastern people, were not there anymore. The ideas that favoured the European People to advance with their armies victoriously into North Africa and Asia no longer existed. The European Monarch was much a despot as his Middle Eastern counterpart. He was as much a tyrant and oppressor as his royal brothers in other parts of the world. Hence, the European armies had lost their advantage over the armies of the East.

The Popes did try to revive European expansion on the lines of Alexander the Great or the Roman Empire by declaring holy wars. However, could not make much difference because the scientific knowledge and thought that is very vital for military success had already been supressed by the Church. Blind faith and ignorance ruled Europe, no one in Europe dared to venture into the world of science due to the fear of persecution.

The Islamic world as a whole did excel in many mathematical and scientific thoughts of the day. Nevertheless, more or less they only grew upon the ideas and books of the ancient philosophers of the Greeks and the Romans. They collected knowledge from the books and knowledge they acquired in the conquered cities like Constantinople and Alexandria. Still, they did better than the Europeans did during these times.

During the end of this period, European people again started to venture into the scientific world. Moreover, European philosophers made philosophical assumptions on the principles of natural sciences and problems of political systems. This made possible due to isolation of Europe from other parts of the world. The parts of the world that infected Europe with a terrible disease of authoritarian political system were no longer able to infect it.

Discovery of the New Worlds and the New World Order

With European expansion stopped or resisted vigorously into North Africa and Asia, new routes were explored and chartered. To make way for expansion of trade and political influence, these naval expeditions were very helpful. During the early modern times, starting around 1500 AD, the European sailors, and seamen did what they were best suited. They undertook voyages into deep seas to find routes towards oriental countries. However, the undertaking of these exercises was not spontaneous or just with a thought of venturing out in the Sea. The voyages undertaken by using knowledge of astronomers and philosophers, that the world was a sphere and they would come back to place they started. All expeditions planned by geographers and by understanding the scientific methods.

As science was developing during these times, it was no surprise that naval exercises would utilize and reap the rewards of the scientific way and lead into the future. Hence, in an effort to discover new trade routes, the discoveries of new worlds were but accidents. The sailors enlarged the world map. In addition, these sailors chartered the routes to the old world, far away from Europe, with a purpose of establishing trade routes.

European world had the desire to take long voyages into the sea and to drift on the waves of the oceans. While other societies of the world made no effort to measure the length and breadth of the world. Other societies in Africa and Asia had no insight or desire to discover new routes and lands. Neither were the people of these societies willing to move out of the lands of their ancestors, especially towards the North and towards the West.

Human migration during the historical times has always been from the North towards the South. Rarely have humans migrated in great numbers from the South towards the North. It is so because human migration from warmer regions into colder climates is a rarity. It somehow prohibited by inbuilt physiological and psychological inhibitions.

The unwillingness of the non-European societies to make inroads into undiscovered parts of the globe was due to some very awkward social customs, if not due to biological restrictions. The societies in Asia and Africa due to invasions of the nomadic tribes into their fertile lands had an inborn fear of the lands beyond the frontiers of their settled kingdoms. Moreover, this fear had come to become hatred after generations of harassment. Due to the fears and the dreads instilled in the settled people of Africa and Asia, the lands beyond the demarcations of the settled life has been considered impure and barbarian. This fear and hatred was one of the main reasons for not making these people especially in China and South Asia venture out of the self-imposed shell, that these people imprisoned themselves.

While in the Middle East all scientific thought borrowed from the Greek and Roman books depleted. In addition, new knowledge did not pour in because of the hostilities between the Islamic Middle East and Christian Europe.

When the European Explorers discovered the new continents of the Americas, the Eastern World had a respite from the incoming and impending attacks it would have suffered. It surely would have, if there were no new lands left in the world to occupy. The social and scientific superiority of the West and the weapons of destruction that these superiorities had inferred to the Western Civilization, the East would have suffered heavily. All Western weapons would have been unleashed on the primitive Eastern nations. Like the Americas, the entire Eastern World would have been another place for the European Nations to populate with their people. In doing so, the West would have wasted much Eastern Life, since no Eastern Nation was capable enough to face or stop the Western onslaught. It would be like Czarist Russia's advance into Central Asia. The Russians marched into Central Asia and routed the nomadic armies without much effort. This proved the superiority of the Western civilization. All Eastern nations would have suffered the same fate if the new world had not existed.

It is just that the energies of the West directed towards the sparsely populated landmasses of the Americas. The destructive powers of its weapons and the march of its armies did not to face the backwardness of the Eastern Societies, especially in the Middle East. This too would have been part of the European hegemony like Africa and South Asia, if the west directed its energy on this part.

One thing that is of great interest is, when the Europeans ventured deep into the African and Asian lands, hence forth unknown to them or known only through tales and stories.

They discovered a society filled with wide spread ignorance and corruption in Asia, with the rulers and upper classes in a well-entrenched position to exploit and use the other classes in the worse manners possible. They found a very under developed society in Africa.

When the period was changing into revival of the old culture of Europe in which science was the tool of reasoning and not religion, the 'Renaissance' of Europe also changed its fortunes. 'Renaissance' coming into Europe was not due to some change in climate or change in the regimes that had ruled Europe in the Dark Ages. Renaissance was the result of the efforts of many people, who had the courage to stand against the absurd teachings of the Church.

Renaissance in Europe was like an evolution of the society. A society that after many trails and errors eventually found a way to make way for a system that was best for carrying forward the progress of man without further escalations of class wars and social inequality. It was just like the evolution of an organism to fit into its environment in changing conditions and challenges.

After the rise of Islam in the Middle East, there was a deep-rooted hatred and aversion between the Christian Europe and the Eastern Islamic World. When the Middle East was not oppressive towards the Europeans and ruled over by European Empires, the influx of Eastern ideas and beliefs had constantly poured into Europe. These ideas were so virulent that the ruling class and the clergy were in fact caught this infection for their own good and indulgences. However, since Islamic and the Christian World detested each other so much, a wall was created between these two worlds. This wall had a height so towering, a thickness too wide, and strength so much in magnitude that this wall did not allow the exchange of ideas between the two different spheres.

It is quite possible that with the Eastern ideas not making their way into the streets and into the homes of the Western World slowly resolved the infection of Eastern thought in Europe, especially regarding governance. This segregation made European society shed the ideas that were not suited to their society's progress and were very Eastern in their conception. These developments in human history also provide us with new ideas regarding human segregation. While in the ancient times water bodies, deserts and mountains were the major reasons of segregation and isolation of different human societies. During these times, one other major cause of human social segregation had come in play. The separation of human society by the virtue of its religion and means through which humans attempt to reach God had become a tool of human hatred and separation.

Various religions of the worlds, practised by different societies, on different geographical regions, may not have taken man near to God. However, religion has definitely played its part in taking man away from man. It has much to do in the enmity between different human social groups.

Unlike Europe, even at this time, the Middle Eastern, South Eastern, Oriental or African societies never evolved beyond a certain point. These societies could never get out of the shell that had encapsulated their thinking patterns. This tendency could not take these societies beyond a certain level of development. The societies in Asia and North Africa never made it out of the medieval age in the spheres of economics, sociology, military, and sciences. Neither could they build upon their ancient knowledge and advance, due to many religious and social barriers. Even Turkey, which is partly in Asia and partly in Europe, could not evolve beyond a certain point to match the other European societies. Due to the restrictive policies of the state, society, religion, and belief in old customs and practices Turkey lagged behind others in Europe. It did not adopt new ideas and innovations from other European neighbours.

When the nomadic Turks annexed the Anatolian lands, they tried to maintain their democratic system. The type of governance they practised during their nomadic past. This was the reason for discipline in its social and military organisations. Nevertheless, with each passing Sultan, the weaknesses of the Eastern Court started to seep into the royalty and down into the ordinary Turk and eventually into the Turkish Empire. The daily system of intrigues and indulgences, ideas of divinity in the crown finally took all democratic institutions out of Turkish Empire's political and administrative system. The Turks lost their advantage over the European kingdoms when they lost their democratic past and swept into the authoritarian system that made Turkey 'The Sick Man of Europe'. That sickness was definitely the contagious disease that Turkey's Ruling Elite had caught from their Eastern and Southern regions and neighbours, especially Baghdad and Isfahan.

This fault has always been responsible for the backwardness of the world beyond the frontiers of Europe. These places, due to some unknown reasons, do not favour a democratic setup, which is very important for a society to evolve. Like the European society, that evolved after the sparks of democratic thought lit during the times of the 'Renaissance'. Maybe, the European Societies were not averse to change. While the other Societies wanted to practice, the same old traditions laid through the centuries by older generations. The societies outside of Europe did not want to change. They were in fact averse to change and progress. They did not want to form a society that could match the changing environment. Like the social evolution in European nations. This evolution came most probably, due to a change in population. This Change brought about, possibly, by the epidemics. This might have changed the demography of Europe and the thinking and behaviour of the population.

The Protestants who separated from the Roman Church or the Vatican were the bringers of change in European Societies. The Protestants were those people, who had the vision and the will to take the people out of darkness. These educated people knew about widespread misuse of religion by the clergy and they did not accept it. There were Monarchs in Europe who too wanted to break free from the control of the Vatican. Because the Catholic Church interfered in the excesses practised in their personal lives. This was a cue and an impetus for the Protestants to speak against the Vatican Church and its strict religious principles, actively supported by some kings.

This led to a freedom to speculate in philosophy of nature and science, to create new ideas, to innovate new mechanisms of scientific progress. Scientific innovation and advancement started to flourish in the European Society. In addition, people indulged in scientific discussions and made scientific societies to interact with one another. Later on, setting up of universities added a great push for the scientific development with great advances in physical and life sciences. This scientific knowledge applied to the science of war to design and manufacture new weapons, an advantage for the European Soldier.

The society of Europe once again started to think on the lines of the Greek and Roman Republics. In addition, the idea of democracy started to spawn in the society of the European Continent once again. So did the idea to limit the powers of the monarchs. The seeds of change, sown in European lands during the early parts of this period made this society roll towards greatness. This ultimately made Europe 'Great' again. Europe came back and evolved on the lines of the Greek Republics and the Roman Empire.

In the rest of the world, the societies of Africa, Asia, and Americas had made no progress. These societies had not developed any mechanism to evolve. The people in these societies lived with the same ideas that their ancestors had lived with, thousands of years ago. They had not developed organised methods of education and governance. These societies still relied on the old principles of politics and social structure. Compared to the European Society, especially of the Central and Western Europe, the Sub-Saharan African communities had not evolved beyond 400 BC or 300 BC. The tribes in the Sub Saharan Africa had not evolved beyond the hunter- gatherer society. Even, the Middle Eastern Societies (North Africa, Asian Islamic World of Western Asia and Central Asia) had inbuilt limitations not to evolve beyond 1600 AD. China of that time was quite backward and it too could not go beyond the culture of 1400 AD. The societies of the South Asia and South East Asia were quite backward and effete. Moreover, these societies too could not evolve beyond the 1300 AD.

It meant that these societies were not willing to evolve. Either the environment surrounding these societies prevented evolution due to some climatic restrictions. On the other hand, these societies themselves were either averse to change or unwilling for progress. They were willing to follow the same customs, followed in the ancient times. They did not find it favourable to change. Alternatively, did not get the opportunity to evolve beyond a certain point due to their geographical locations and isolation.

Whatever the reasons, progress of these societies remained stagnant until the arrival of the Europeans or the Westerners. The Europeans sailed on the waves of the high seas and took these societies by surprise. The Westerners surprised by the relative poor progress of the societies in Africa and Asia looked down upon the people of these lands.

The other reason for this stagnation, if the climatic conditions were not responsible, could be biochemical changes induced in the humans living on the temperate lands of Europe. A certain biochemical change in the genetic structure of humans in Europe prompted the European Society to evolve from time to time to cope with the changings of times. Such genetic changes did not throw up in other societies, the ones outside of Europe. Due to which they could not and 'cannot' evolve beyond a certain point in time. If these societies can evolve and change with the needs of time that change is very slow. Then it is also possible that non-European Societies do not evolve as quickly as the European society does. Hence, the non-European social setup loses in the race of social evolution.

The pattern of evolution of these societies is very different from the European social evolution. In addition, the tidings of time shall render these groups obsolete.

One thing that is of great interest is, when the Europeans ventured deep into the African and Asian Lands, henceforth unknown to them. They discovered a society filled with wide spread corruption and stratification in Asia. It was easy for the Europeans to imagine that they could with time, overcome these corrupt people. The people infected by every moral and social corruption that there was. The Asian countries were scientifically backward, with very little military technology development. The people were embroiled in every social evil and superstition. In addition, these things were the cause of their primitiveness.

African people too were in a tribal set up. The tribes were jealous of one another. Moreover, there was no development of society on scientific lines. The military prowess of the African People was not organised even in the smallest, compared with the European Powers.

The Americas and Australian landmasses became new havens for European Culture. While North America and Australia were in time to become part of the Western Democratic Institution. These places paced ahead of Europe at times in new forms of governments and democratic rights. The rights handed down to every section of society in slow, controlled phases down the years. The Indigenous American people, compared to the Europeans were much lower on the scale of social development. In addition, whatever Europeans brought to the continent meant death in the form of communicable diseases, war, and slavery. In a matter of time, these people completely lost their culture to the

Europeans. In addition, whosoever survived the harshness of history mixed with the ever-growing European Population and became Americanised or Latinised.

Similar was the truth about the Australian Aboriginals, who too suffered greatly at the hands of the early settlers from Europe. Sensing inherent weaknesses in these primitive societies the Europeans easily overpowered these continents and started making these countries their colonies. The colonies became supplies of raw material to power the factories in European homelands. Moreover, without exception the Europeans too exploited the local population. This exploitation was somewhat similar to the way their own folk and rulers exploited these people, before the coming of the Europeans into these worlds.

The European Armies, well-disciplined and well drilled, equipped with state of the art weaponry and an established chain of command, with assured supplies and a system that could withstand political turmoil without breaking up, were more than a match for the ancient battle tactics of the African and Asian people. The Eastern armies were nothing more than armed gangs were. Hence, the period of supremacy of the European system of government over the rotten systems that prevailed at the times in other continents commenced.

At the start of the early modern age around about 1500 AD, winds of change were blowing in Europe. The winds brought change because the written word in the Bible reached the common people in Europe. The Bible translated into nearly all the European languages. It spread light among the ignorant common Europeans. At first The Bible, written and preached in the Latin language, a select few read Latin in Europe. However, due to the efforts of the Protestants and other reformers, enlightened people wrote the Bible in all the local alphabets and disseminated it into the public. This effort of the reformers did limit the authority of the Church. Because the common folk who could read and write, now became aware of what their religion said. In addition, the people now were not dependent on the Church to interpret the religion for them.

This led to drastic changes in the European society. As the persecution, lessened and scientific knowledge began to flower in the social circles of illustrated Europeans. Advancements in science during this time brought about military machines into battle use. This brought advancements in agriculture. Biological sciences and physical sciences began to answer questions that benefitted society as a whole. However, even this did not bring in political change. However, even all this did put the European powers at an advantage over their competitors present elsewhere.

The industrialization of Europe had also started due to the spread of education among the masses. In addition, with affluent families sent their children to schools and universities. This was a step away from the time when affluent people leisured their time with hunting and sporting events.

Every decade, a new thought penetrated into the minds of the people and there reached a time when they wanted to limit the powers of the Monarchs. In addition, slowly they succeeded in diluting the powers of the monarch. Especially, those powers of the rulers that dealt with taxation that made people unhappy. Once done, the people wanted to limit the Monarchs ever more, which at times the monarchs resisted.

At times, the rulers had to give in to the popular demands or lost their heads from their bodies.

However, as time went forward, the European population swelled. However, this swelling of population meant more hands for working on the fields and more inflow of food and money. Nevertheless, this process increased the greed of landowners and the rulers. Who wanted absolute control over the serfs and treated these people like chattel. The serfs were nothing more than industrial assets for the landowners, those assets that generated revenue in the form of grain and vegetables. As the population increased, so did food for them. Nevertheless, the landowners wanted a lion's share in the produce harvested on their fields and this led to trouble.

First of all the villages, towns, and cities overflowed with people. Secondly, these townships did not have the hygienic conditions that were required for the people. The cities' planning was not on scientific principles. Nor had these cities developed in accordance with hygiene. This condition was present in all the towns and cities of Europe. All this was a brewing ground for an upcoming epidemic. Moreover, it was most probably spreading upwards from Asia. The Asian population too was living in these same miserable conditions and it still is living in these medieval conditions.

Certain natural calamities, coupled with political reasons led to some very severe and politically explosive conditions in Europe around 1800 AD. Human disease, failure of harvests due to weather and plant diseases all combined in freeing the European serfs from their bonds. Education among sections of society who were neither too poor nor to rich or powerful provided the impetus necessary for the coming of change on European lands.

Many writers and educated people were not too happy by the power and wealth enjoyed by the nobility in Europe. These educated people believed that the wealth of a nation meant to provide for good of the state and the people as a whole. The squandering of a nation's wealth by a select few with the aim of indulgence did not go down in their educated and newly developed thoughts.

The nobility on the other had did not want to let go of the power that they enjoyed over the workers and the peasants. Hence, a situation of discontent was brewing up in every section of society in Europe. Harsh weather conditions during these times led to poor harvests, the population of Europe had increased substantially during these times. Moreover, the fiery writings in the books had charged the mind of young people into a revolutionary mode. Needed were a few cruel steps by the monarchs. The rest of the material for revolutionary change was already present in environment.

It could also be possible that the plagues of the past had virtually wiped out the submissive gene pool from the European population. The people of these times were a population quite different from the ones that lived in Europe during the medieval times. These people were more resistant to disease and more ready to fight for equality and dignity. Whatever the causes, the people of Europe raised up against the oppressive system. They changed the political face of Europe quickly and efficiently. In addition, they paved for a future that led to a democratic form of government and human progress, especially in the Western World.

It was something that had happened on no other continent and never before in history. The people rose up and made the Monarchs tremble and shake underneath their crowns. It also made the rulers realize that people were supreme. Moreover, repressive measures for political control and administration if used again might prove dangerous. Governments realized that effective administrative changes were required lest the people might behead the rulers.

The revolutions that happened in Europe slowly and steadily increased the pace of development in society and political system in Europe. These social changes gave the people rights over their lives. The rulers tried to provide people with good government policies so as not to offend the people in to another uprising. Hence, the sweet fruit of democracy brought inside Europe, slowly eroded the powers of the autocracy. Moreover, this change ushered a time of prosperity and progress into the European society.

If during these times, European military power and its scientific thought were at the top of the world. It was only due to the political freedom, and democratic set up that was laying its foundations in Europe. Without it, Europe would have been no better than any other continent of the time. Democratic practices made the governments realize what the people wanted. In addition, this meant progress and peace in society because popular feelings were not hurt.

The most important thing that brought democracy in the Western Society was the spirit of nationalism. Moreover, it was the most important spirit that bound someone to the place of one's living, to think of it as one's home. This also meant that the people worked together to protect their homeland. In addition, to make it a better place for their coming generations. This spirit of nationalism was the creation of democratic practices. Without democracy, nationalism could never raise its head above the ground.

By 1900 AD, Europe had overshadowed every corner of the globe populated by humans. The pace of industrialization, militarisation, and infrastructure development undertaken in Europe was unsurpassed in history. If Europe wanted, then it could trample the entire world beneath the march of its soldiers. However, the jealously that European Powers had for each other was also their unbecoming. Their jealousies meant destruction and decimation for each other. While the rest of the world watched, European nations bombarded each other's homes. They used new type of bombs, gassed each other's young men with innovative chemicals of annihilation. They blew up the cities that dotted Europe for the love of destruction and hate for each other. European powers tried all mechanisms to downsize each other. They deployed all ways of force and methods of subjugation equally deployed. However, with all the devastation caused, it still came to naught. the European nations after all the wastage of ammunition, metal and most of all the lives of its denizens returned back to the cause of building nations without achieving anything.

The major cause of jealousy was definitely that some European powers had established colonies in the third world countries and some could not. The ones who had established colonies vehemently stopped those who could not. The major reason of this was that the countries who had established colonies in the third world did not want other countries of Europe to reap the benefits of the relative weaknesses of third world nations and exploit their backwardness.

If 1800 AD was the coming of age for Europe then 1900 AD was the end of European hegemony and it was due to European firepower and destructive capabilities. The European hegemony on the world caused a series of conflicts inside Europe itself. With lots of political manoeuvring, that came into play to keep each other engaged in trivial matters.

This led to the first Great War, which although not that widespread, was great enough to engulf Europe, and the Middle East within its flames. The destruction that this war brought was great indeed and showed the destructive power of science and technology to the world. Europe could make use of military power it possessed, for the progress and spread of its civilization. The firepower that Europe had, its people could use outside the European Continent, to bring democracy and world peace on the entire globe. However, it's people used inside it for their own doom.

The First Great War is a classical case that shows the flaws in an authoritarian system and superiority of a system that is more democratic, federal, and less repressive. The first Great War was a clash between the ideas of Western Europe and Central-Eastern Europe. The Western European culture has given the world a system of governance that is localised or decentralised. The Americans amplified this system further and made it complete with much checks and balances on the central authority.

The political systems adopted by the Prussians or The Austro-Hungarian Empire, the Turks or the Russians are centralised systems. The central authority has much power. This system may have the inherent capability to introduce militarism in a society. Nevertheless, it cannot run a society on all parameters.

During the initial period of the First Great War, no doubt the Central Powers made great successes. These initial pushes by the Central Powers' armies were due to usual vigour of a military state. However, as the war raged on the centralized political system of the Central Powers became to crumble in front of the unrepressed, localised system in which the common people participated actively.

While in the centralized system, it is the governments that take up the cause of the nations, in a localised system the people take up the cause of the government. More people are involved in running and ensuring the success of a federal and a localised system. While very, few people bear the burden of a centralised system. Prolonged conflict clearly showed the superiority of the federal and localised system. The centralised system lost due to the fatigue that it gave itself when faced with the ever evolving and adapting federal and localised political system.

After the Second Great War, the colonies left to fend for themselves. It showed the true administrative qualities of the Western civilization. The local tribes and monarchs managed the Third World very badly. The population of Third World Nations were living in a pit of ignorance, darkness, surrounded by superstitions and unpractical social practices that never let their society develop into an organised system. Democracy for these nations was impossible notion. If these nations ever governed themselves properly and efficiently, it was during the European hegemony.

Before the Europeans arrived in the Third World, a hierarchy of people, one above the other, exploited its nation's population. The people of these nations were in majority poor and living under terrible conditions. After a time under European Rule, there was law and order in these nations, with an efficient police network for keeping peace in the colonies. Law and order brought stability for the colonies and finally an increase in trade and commerce, this ushered prosperity in these colonies. The people of the colonies prospered under the European rule, many infrastructural projects laid out in these nations for the improvement of trade. The laying of railroads and the digging up of the irrigation canals was some of the most important developmental works.

The colonies due to their latitudes on the global map were all sub-tropical or tropical. They had the resources that European Lands did not have. To utilize those resources to the fullest the factories that could process these raw resources were located in Europe. European Hegemony in the colonies fully utilized these natural blessings of the colonies. The European companies and traders made use of these resources for their individual selves. This also helped make their companies and their nations rich and upbeat. While those nations who did have access to the East were much jealous of the nations who had ventured out in the seas and had carved out a place outside Europe for their prosperity.

These modern activities were unthinkable under self-rule of the colonies. Moreover, for the first time the affluent people of the colonies became educated outside their religious studies with the spread of the printing press. The European rule of these times was in fact the best times that the people of the Third World Countries had ever experienced. Because with organised government machinery, the scope for trade and commerce too increased. In addition, the colonies prospered for the first time in a long time of existence.

European rule also meant fewer invasions and hence less turmoil, due to which the colonies flourished and bloomed with new vigour once unknown in these parts. With new planned towns, agriculture network, and industrial enterprises that had come up in the colonies. It was a new beginning for the people of these countries. The colonies flourished for a long time as the Europeans trained and armed the people under their leadership and enlisted them in their armies. It meant negligible invasions on the colonies by raiders and hence a time to prosper for a long time in peace.

However, the Second Great War ended all this. Adolf Hitler in his rage and hate for the Western Powers may ultimately have taken Germany towards defeat. Nevertheless, all the destruction that was started by the Axis and finally ended by Allies meant an end of European Hegemony and freedom for its colonies. The brunt of destruction borne by Europe was unthinkable. With a third of European population destroyed by the explosive power of science that rained from the heavens, the oceans and the ground alike, it drained itself. The nations of Central Europe, along with Japan were authoritative states. They raised their military for making war, but they did not raise their civilization to prepare for war.

Their excessive militarization in contrast to the democratic system of the Western European Nations could never survive a long conflict due to allocation of resources and division of labour. The Allies won again just due to the form of government that their society practised. Their society was better suited to handle the conflict due to their form of government. The Germans did not learn from their defeat in the First War and did not render their centralized system obsolete. The Second Great War also showed the advantage of the federal, localised democracy in favour of a centralized political system, whether democratic or dictatorship.

The Western World, especially Europe has yet even after decades since the Second World War not fully recovered from the shock that this terrible conflict gave to the nations dotted on the map of Europe. Moreover, it will take many years still until Europe makes a full recovery and becomes the ancient power that it once was. That is, if it does not meet the same fate again, through the same means and under the same circumstances that gave it the two 'Great Wars'.

However, so much destruction as Europe had faced in the Second Great War, the decimation of a large number of its people, it was nearly impossible for the Colonial Powers to establish control over their subject colonies effectively. The Colonial Powers had to undertake reconstruction of their own homelands. In addition, at the same time exercise their dominance over their colonies. It was a daunting task. The Colonial Powers thought it better to reconstruct their own countries rather than carry on in the subject colonies with an under staffed government. Faced with acute shortage of work force back home the European Powers decided to pull out of the third world countries. They had to call in immigrants from all over the world to help the Europeans to rebuild their bombed cities.

It was the belief with the European Leaders that the incoming workforce and their families, in time, would be Europeanised or Westernised. Their new generations would forget about their culture and social practices. However, that has not happened altogether. Because the cultures and social practices too are part of the evolutionary, process and deeply imbedded into ones genetic makeup. The social behaviours can change through the dilution of the genetic structure, through inbreeding. Otherwise, the social behaviours are difficult to modify by a mere change of environment. No immigrants from other nations have given up their social practices after settling in Europe after the Second World War. As it is visible in the present European Nations, that have brought in large number of immigrants. Rather the immigrants try to enforce their cultural norms on the society that brought these immigrants into this part of the world.

In nearly all the places that the Europeans occupied and annexed in the third world, they left an organised and efficient system and institution of administration. This could immensely benefit the third world colonies if the people of these colonies wanted. Eventually the Europeans handed political power to the local people of the colonies. They established self-rule for the local populations and left for their homelands, one after the other. No European colonies remained in the third world, barring a few after 1960 AD.

Nevertheless, the time after the Great War was a time when scientific and technological advances took place in a pace too quick. All the technologies invented by the Axis or Allied Powers. Those technologies that gave them an advantage over each other in war for destruction, they reused.

They ultimately used in power generation, industrialization, physiological sciences, and civil engineering to make the Western Society excel once more.

Japan was the only exception in the Third world. It had the mind and the will to hold its head high among the Western World and at times much higher than the Western Economies. Because Japan had understood, how the European nations had progressed and became super powers. The Japanese ruling class had the determination to push their nation into industrialization. They wanted to change the obsolete social customs that could never let Japan come out of the medieval times.

After the Second Great war, the world division based on political systems again helps in acknowledging the superiority of the federal, localised system of administration. The division of the world into the Eastern and Western Blocs provides insights into the weakness of the centralized systems.

USSR was a centralised state, in fact, it was heavily centralized, and the central authorities took every small decision. This overburdened the government of USSR's leadership; it involved it in matters best handled by local decision makers. The central authorities were not aware of the ground realities that prevailed in their nation. The central leadership, surrounded by their guards and their protocols were far from the people. The low rung officers ignored and exploited the people under the communist regime. The general population hated the leadership. This one big mistake made the USSR fall on its own weight.

The Western Bloc right from the beginning was at an inherent advantage over the Eastern Bloc. The two Great

Wars, and the Cold War; all won by it on the shoulders of its federal localised system of administration. The system best suited to adjust according to the fluctuations within a society.

By the 1970 when the Western Economies were advancing their society rapidly. The Third World left by the Europeans, was slowly going down to the same level it once was, before the European Hegemony. The democratic values in the Third World slowly decay and give in to the authoritarian regimes and governments. It has been an inherent weakness of the Third World that it cannot support a healthy democratic setup and democratic institutions. In the third World, the people want an autocratic or an authoritarian system. A system that is unfair and unjust for the people who are far from political power. A group of individuals for their own self-interests easily hijacks such systems.

Each passing day of the gone colonial hegemony brought in decay for democracy in the Third World. Political power corrupted the people who had gained or wrested power in the Third World. Because these political leaders have an illiterate population to rule over who are unaware of their rights. They had a population that had no knowledge of the institution of democracy. Moreover, individual freedom was beyond their grasp. These people were active supporters of crony capitalism and monopolistic business practices. This system made some rich while most poor. There became visible an ever growing trench between the rich and the poor in the Third World, due to these policies.

In such systems, for the detection and prevention of crime the police have no role. However, for political repression of political enemies and those who do not acknowledge the present rulers, the police are an effective tool of repression. Such practices eventually led to widespread economic mismanagement. Ultimately, no Third World Countries ever recovered from the discrepancies that its own people created among its population.

By the end of 1999 AD, the third world countries were dependent on aids by the Western economies. Their cities are in dilapidated conditions. These countries had badly managed health system and crony capitalism at its peak. These systems also led to less job opportunities for the young. Moreover, these political systems promoted protection for established industrial companies. New job producing businesses were few to arise due to such policies that prevented healthy business competition.

Such systems prevented new people to set up industrial projects that could provide employment for their ever-growing population. It was a process carried out at the behest of already established industrialized families. They wanted monopolistic control in a nations market. The political people who were in power in each successive regime and gained wealth through these policies for themselves and their families supported such political policies. While their brethren suffered, the political class successfully supported this policy.

One of the most interesting aspects of all this observation is that the administration kept law and order efficiently during European Hegemony. Nevertheless, later on the politics of these countries especially in Asia is a classic example of Machiavellian politics. Politicians indulged in intrigues and schemes for gaining power and retaining it by befooling the people who exercise their suffrage.

Unemployment among the third world countries was very little and was not such bothersome issue under the European Rule, as it is today. Crony capitalism in these Third World Countries is also responsible for widespread pollution in their townships. This is created by unchecked industrial effluents and littering of garbage that in time shall have great consequences for these countries. Somehow, populations of the Third World Countries appreciate this unjust system because of their submissive nature. This enforced by political repression. It is a property in their character handed over to them through centuries of human development and evolution.

By 2000 AD, the West had proved in some military exploits that that they were a force to reckon with. No nation in the third world that could challenge the west in any sphere be it war or during the times of peace. New weapon technology shown to the world in the wars in the decades of late 1900 AD and early 2000 AD has made the East fear the West once again. It proved that the West has developed its society for future development of human progress and ingenuity. Nevertheless, this development has come through its democratic institutions. It is coming out of the shock that it suffered during the Second World War. The Third World has not capitalized on the gains that the colonial rulers had provided for the colonies. The Eastern world is devolving and losing out to the Western world, except Japan and maybe China.

THE MAP OF WORLD POLITICAL SYSTEMS

The political systems of humans are easily visible on the map according to the various geographical locations. Certain geographies and ethnicities seem to favour certain type of political systems. This justifies that that governance has a link with biological organisation of humans. Hence, political systems are biological decisions. In addition, it is difficult to change political behaviours of various social groups or cultures through other interventions.

If historical times are considered, all geographical areas of the world started with a tribal set up. This set up was somewhat similar in all social groups, no matter where they lived. Then City –States arose in the Middle East and South Asia. These City-States most probably arose on the shores of shallow seas created by the receding glaciers. In most probability, these City-States were creations of a foreign element superimposed on indigenous population. This foreign element emigrated from Europe, just like the Vikings. The ideas of Kingship spread through these City-States. As times crept towards the modern ages Europe developed republics. North Africa and Asia drifted towards large empires while rest of the world remained tribal.

Throughout history, many fluctuations have taken place in political system of Western Europe, Central Part of Europe, and Some Parts of Eastern Europe. Rest of the World has not tried to resist or change their political systems. In other parts of the World, people have lived happily or unhappily under the same system until the Europeans forcibly made these people change their governance methods during the early modern times. Later on, these nations retained the political systems due to fears of overwhelm by the Western nations. Some nations reverted to their traditional monarchical through force of arms.

While Europe first opted for a republican system, it later diverted towards the Eastern form of political practices that took Europe into the Dark Ages. Later on it were the European populations that decided to overthrow this cruel and oppressive system, through dissents and revolutions through centuries. However, the European common people succeeded in reverting to their ancient system, that of democracy. While the Eastern people made no efforts regarding this. The European population made a change that was very different from rest of the human population.

The world division into various sectors and blocs according to the forms of governments that various populations of humans 'love' is easy to judge. Europe too, has political divisions. The Western part of Europe is federal and its political powers spread locally into towns and cities. Central European nations have a tendency to lean towards a centralized system. That tendency increases much more and becomes authoritarian in Eastern Europe.

In the Middle East, people are seeking a powerful leader and have leaning towards a very authoritarian type of political system. Moreover, it extends to most countries that have an Islamic majority. This tendency is part of this population since first kingdoms came on up on its soils and its sands. The Southern Asian People too favour an authoritarian type of government. Democracy is beyond their intellect and scope of thought.

The Mongoloid people have a strong tendency to support an authoritarian type of government. Nevertheless, the Northern parts of the Mongoloid world are more leant towards this system than the Southern part.

In the modern times, political division has clearly separated the world into various political systems. Some of these political systems will ultimately finish or other systems will assimilate them. After these political entities, destroy themselves through mismanagement. As a system does not destroy itself, mismanagement slows its progress. It is a slow form of degradation. It slowly crumbles a system on its own weight, until overwhelmed by a foreign element. Others shall clash and ultimately the Western system, the one that is federal, decentralized, and localized shall ultimately finish the authoritarian centralized systems, where such systems exist. The Western system shall triumph the way it emerged victorious during the two Great Wars and the Cold War. It is a lesson learnt from history and it is going to happen, for sure.

LESSONS LEARNT FROM HISTORY

Prehistory and History of Human Civilization has provided enough lessons. Lessons learnt from the past to improve the future of the human world. However, not all societies are ready to improve the future of their children in some proven ways. While some societies have recognised the importance of improvement in their surroundings, some have not. Other societies are quite primitive or unevolved for this betterment. Though they realize, that if they do not act it shall be disastrous for them.

Long time after humans migrated from their site of origin to every place that could provide them foothold. They have made it their home. Nevertheless, by spreading to different parts of the world, humanity has diverged into many different forms and shapes. The long distances between various human societies and the natural boundaries or barriers that have separated these societies have not created enough differences among all the human races. These differences are not impossible barriers that work to prevent the efforts to unite human race into one. These barriers are not that strong, as to prevent the mixing of one race with another. Moreover, create a single race with similar exterior features and internal biochemical environments. Nevertheless, it shall never happen that way. Different human races want to evolve into different directions from one another. Ultimately, there shall be one human race that shall occupy the planet. From the current sway of events, the Caucasian race shall eventually be the dominant human race. It shall assimilate the other human races, whatever trace elements that shall survive.

Climate and environment has changed humans into many diverse forms. These differences are not only exterior or cosmetic. The changes in skin colour, eye pigment, hair texture, and facial characteristics are due to many internal changes that are not discernible to the human eye. Changes in genetic structure and internal chemicals that have changed the exterior appearance of human body have changed many other things. In addition, the way these different human races plan and think.

Creation of races during the course of time, when the shallow seas separated the humans has diversified humans. Those seas that invaded the lands between various continents after the ice age are responsible for much of the racial differences. Moreover, these prevented human interbreeding for a very long time. In addition, were in fact responsible for the evolution of different cultures. Different human races during their period of segregation opted for those social practises that they found suitable for their existence and for the betterment of their collections or tribes.

Cultural changes induced into various human races by the pressures of environment through the centuries. It is not only difficult but also impossible to change certain societies to mould into social experiments and cultural confines of some other society. This is why some societies have not understood the changing concept of governance and social setup. Those introduced by the Western nations into other parts of the world in the present times. Due to their superior military technology and organised civil structure, this made the Europeans conquer the primitive societies. Which the societies outside of Europe could not develop due to the way these societies had evolved through the centuries.

Democratic institutions developed during ancient times in perhaps all tribal societies of humans. Where the division of labour had separated men and women to indulge in certain activities handed out to them. However, this happened under the supervision of their chiefs and elders.

Nevertheless, as humans evolved, some of them were in a better position to take advantage of others or live off the work of others of their kind. In addition, this must have created a ruling class and the priestly class. These two classes have enjoyed the fruits of civilization for a long time, right from the beginning until the modern times. Moreover, this must be the reason for abolishing democracy from within the tribe. As its members grew in numbers or many tribes assimilated into larger societies as they became monarchies.

There have been, through historical times, many discrepancies between the ruling class and the subject masses. Especially in societies that had evolved beyond tribal setups. Moreover, all of them were outside Europe. The ruling classes might have been physically different from the subjects in such societies. In addition, the immigrants were most probably from the colder lands of the European continent. If such big differences did not exist during ancient times between the rulers and the subjects, it was in Europe only. Due to similar characteristics of the European population and because they looked alike it was viable in Europe.

In larger societies and cities in the ancient times, the practise of democracy prevailed only in the republics of Southern Europe. In addition, certain Aryan entities that had setup kingdoms elsewhere. When these people immigrated out of Europe into the Middle East and South Asia and set up kingdoms there. After some time such republics no longer existed outside Europe or they changed their methods of governance. Therefore, democracy during ancient times was a European concept. Moreover, people of similar ethnicity and similar social standing practised democratic governments. Tribes that ruled over other ethnic groups did not practise it. Most of the ruling elite that ruled over people in North Africa and Asia have been invaders coming out of Europe or Central Asia. Hence, they never wanted to practise democracy in their kingdoms. If they did, they could not exploit their indigenous subjects. They were physically and habitually very different from the rulers. Therefore, when the world or some societies of the world emerged out of the tribe into bigger conglomerate of people, democracy was no longer viable for any other part of the globe except Europe.

The foreign rulers and their kin slowly mixed with the indigenous populations. However, the ideas regarding kingship did not dilute. Anyone who was strong enough to take over and sit on the throne became authoritarian, supported by the priestly class. The subjects due to some inherent attitude that was part of their mind and body welcomed it. The subject ethnic groups never resisted such practises.

Maybe the lands that had many foreign invaders, like North Africa, Western Asia, Southern Asia, developed a stratification of society. Moreover, each successive wave of invader placed itself above the other. This excessive stratification through the past could be responsible for the authoritarian governments that the people of the Eastern World support and sustain until this day.

If the Eastern People, the majority of them, are in fact not in favour of an authoritarian government to rule their society, no power on Earth can establish such a government midst their cultures. Sadly, the majority of the Eastern people, in fact, are in favour of such governments. This is the reason that these governments exist in the first place, else the majority would have overthrown the yoke of authoritarians. The majority would have endeavoured to establish a system that was more caring for the needs and progress of Eastern societies.

Long distance travel too was an invention of the European tribes. Who were the most probable originators of the early river valley civilizations? These civilisations imparted much to the development of the Eastern people. However, with the passage of time the Early River Valley Civilizations' people inbred with indigenous people. In addition, the ruling class of these cities, who in time had lessened their European blood, slowly lost their ancient knowledge and capabilities of management. In addition, they turned to the social structure and living attitude as designed to live by the Eastern evolutionary pattern. This happened when land routes opened, after the inland seas dried up.

At this time, the Aryan People or the horse riding people rode out of Europe. They spread new ideas into the minds of the people whom they conquered and into whom they assimilated. They changed the demography of most of the Middle East, Central Asia, and South Asia. In addition, they assimilated into the Mongoloid People and created a new culture in the Eastern Part of Asia. Chinese civilization took to building cities quite late, the same time when the Aryans emigrated out of Europe.

Scientific thought too was the creation of the European Mind. When the Aryans made their homes far away from Europe this scientific thought spread among the Eastern Populations. Moreover, this European emigration was instrumental for advancement of the human civilization, as one society grew on the ideas of the other.

From these incidents and historical events placed before us. It is quite clear that major ideas of change spread from Europe into rest of the world through immigrations and invasions. However, few ideas travelled from the Eastern world into the European lands. If the west received ideas from the east, the European People improved upon those ideas, like the use of gunpowder for defence and offence. In addition, the spread of these new ideas after a brief respite were enough to change the society. Moreover, raise it above the previous level so that the world in essence evenly developed from the west to the east.

During the ancient times, the spirit of republicanism and philosophy that was the hallmark of the Latin Cultures was a great step in the evolution of the European Society. Nevertheless, these inceptions of Latin Society were only possible because of a society's exposure to many new cultures that surrounded it. Because the European Tribes living in isolation in the deeper parts of Europe were immune to these republican ideas shows the need for exposure. The interior lands of Europe were the breeding grounds from where republican ideas emerged. In addition, these people amplified the republican or democratic ideas, when they settled in the Mediterranean.

From this, it is quite clear that for evolution and progress of human society exposure to different cultures is very necessary. Because the cultures not exposed to competition were the ones that had not evolved in line with the cultures that had gone through competition. Cultures exposed to competition developed with quickness and in complexity in relation to the primitive cultures that had evolved in relative or complete isolation.

It is of great interest to note that for reasons known or unknown, the evolved societies had fair skins. That is, these societies, mutated from their original human forms due to the environment of extreme cold during the ice ages. These races, forced through competition against the environment developed some characteristics that dark skinned populations could not. The primitive societies consisted of the darker coloured humans, having the original human form. Moreover, in relativity the light coloured human races evolved faster than dark races even in the ancient times and gradually built upon their past successes to outshine the darker races. While the darker races remained stagnant, did not evolve and progress. They never built upon their past successes to create a civilization that could surpass the achievements of the light-skinned humans. It means that the fair-skinned races developed or evolved from the races, which were relatively dark but either the deletion of some chemicals from their bodies or the addition of some made them different. These light-skinned humans became different not only in their visible form but also in their internal chemical form, they had a changed thinking pattern from the original humans. Could it be possible that the mutations thrown up in the human species were responsible for the advancement of fairer human races? On the other hand, some form of interbreeding with some distant human sub species could be responsible for this trait of social development among the mutated people that made them more advanced.

It is a known fact that all animals evolve through mutations. Moreover, for the human evolution that mutation took place in the colder, ice-covered regions of Europe. Along with the accompanying biochemical, changes had made some human races evolve faster than the other races. The mutations that made the Caucasian race have slowly made it spread. The Caucasian culture right from the start of history is trying to enforce itself on other human races.

The Caucasians have always tried to come out of Europe to rule over the world. They are in a constant race with time to populate the whole of the world. The European races, mainly from the colder parts of Europe have a tendency to come out of their cold homes and conquer all in their path. It has happened throughout history except the dark ages. However, even during the dark ages they tried and failed because they lived with Eastern ideas of ignorance. The mutations that changed the humans in Europe to this new form have given this particular race the thought to progress and to spread its seeds to every corner of the globe. It would have been possible if the European races had chosen not to destroy each other during the wars of the early modern times and the two world wars. Nevertheless, it still is a habit among these people to move out Europe whenever their numbers permit and spread their race. It happened during the Aryan migrations and all the invasions that Europeans have undertaken to move out of Europe and destroy all other cultures in their wake. In doing so, they have infused their blood among the people of other races. They have also finished some races, altogether. Like the Austroloid races that populated much of the Middle East, Southern Central Asia and North Western South Asia.

During the ancient times, transmission of all ideas of progress started from the Northern hemisphere, inhabited by the fair and mutated people into the Eastern People who were dark or less mutated. Slow mixture eventually changed much of the populations of the African and Asian lands along with their behaviours regarding social structure along with their blood. From this it is quite clear that only those societies prosper that have equality among its population and those that have inequality and divisions progress with slow time-consuming pace. This equality was present in Europe.

When democratic practices ceased to exist on all places of the evolved world, those societies that had practised democracy lost their advantage over the ones who did not. All were on the same development pattern no matter on which continent. However, during these times the nomadic societies who were democratic had a military edge over the authoritarian kingdoms.

During the medieval times, European ideas were limited to Europe only. Moreover, the religious barriers prevented European ideas from reaching other societies due to the wall of enmity between the Christian Europe and The

Islamic Middle East. They were equally matched in social strengths be it military or administrative. The evolution of the Eastern Societies came to a halt and the Eastern Societies remained stagnant for centuries due to this wall. Moreover, it was impossible for these societies to go beyond a certain point of progress. During the end of this time, the human civilization had different rates of evolution due to no exchange of ideas between Europe and rest of the world. While Europe excelled in scientific thought, the rest of the world could not. Because it no longer had access to new European ideas, as they were receiving during the ancient times. The written knowledge of the European Philosophers did not disperse among the Eastern People, during these times.

However, when the European Nations gained an upper hand over the Islamic World due to the coming of renaissance and through their deep-sea voyages, they changed the world. The evolution of the other societies sped up due to their interaction with the European Sailors. Later on their social development enlarged due to their interactions with the European armies and eventually due to European administration.

During the times of European Hegemony over the world, the pace of social development picked up in the South Asian and Far Eastern Countries. These regions had lagged much behind in development even from the Middle Eastern Society. Moreover, eventually these societies overtook the Middle Eastern society due to active participation of the European rulers, who took the colonies out of the 'Dark Ages'.

After the European Colonial Rulers left these colonies, they established self-rule for the colonial people. These colonies were not in a position to sustain the development or maintain the infrastructure that the Europeans had provided to their colonies. The thought process of the people of the colonies had not developed on European lines. This was very essential, as the European People had developed these colonies on European principles of development. Moreover, for their development the policies implemented too were European. The essence and meaning of these policies was very difficult for the Eastern people of the colonies to understand and implement.

The idea of nation building, which was a creation of the European mind, never developed in the Eastern mind. For the Eastern Mind the nation building mechanism is discrete and is limited to one's family and relatives. Hence, its implementation according to the European Model is beyond the grasp of the Eastern Mind. The political leaders of the Eastern nations, barring Japan, are not interested in distributing the wealth of their nation evenly into the population. It is an Eastern vice to keep ones brother poor so that he may come begging.

The nation building process, in the Eastern Mind has to develop on other lines and not necessarily on the lines of the European Thinkers. This is making development in the Third World difficult. Even during the early times, when the self-rule established in the colonies. After the Europeans left and a long-time after the colonial period swept into the past, the Western World was growing on its older concepts of development and progressing. While, the colonies struggled to cope and live up to the European model of development the Western progressed with those same ideas. The Western World, moved forward, making innovations in social development for the betterment of its 'basic units' the people. The peoples' combined efforts are responsible for the progress of any social entity and it shows in the Western world.

From all this it is quite evident that progress in human civilization from the past times to the present directed from the European lands into other continents. It spread, especially from the lands of Western Europe. Then it dispersed among the Eastern People through travel, immigration, and invasion. When it was impossible for the knowledge to spread, due to whatever circumstances, the evolution of Eastern Societies ceased. The Eastern world no longer received ideas for progress, which it has always received from the West.

It is also evident, that for human society to progress in all spheres it is mandatory that democracy be the form of government in a society. It is much superior to the authoritarian governments. Authoritarian political system depletes a society off its vitality. Moreover, ceases its progress by supressing freethinking, spirit of enterprise and innovation. Eventually it makes the people ignorant. This is very harmful for economic development of any nation.

The Western nations have recognised the problems that the societies of the past have faced and tried to find remedies for making their societies free from such problems in the future. For this, they have created permanent institutions and have put every effort that these institutions remain permanent with new additions progressively. Nevertheless, these Western Nations have also made it a policy not to weaken these institutions at all costs. Lest their society fails or falls and it is such implanted in the Western mind. Evolution has forced the population of these nations to think on this pattern, instinctively.

The Western World concept of policing and justice system evolved first for the protection of the ruling elite. Nevertheless, at the same its purpose for settling the dispute of their subjects and for the prevention of crime among the general population became important. However, its evolution was local. Each town and city had its own system of Mayoralties and shrievalties. This created for individual human settlements, villages, towns, and cities. Since it was a local entity under the protection of the crown, it had the power to be tyrannical towards the common people in the matters of protection of interests of the ruler but on a local level. Nevertheless, this system was quite efficient at the local level during the periods of renaissance and after the evolution of nationalism. One had to go through a democratic process to attain these offices because much power of the social development and maintenance of law and order was in the hands of these offices. Popular support was definitely required to hold these offices in this process. People of nefarious characters could usually not make it to these offices after democratic elections for attaining these offices became mandatory.

Law and Order improved due to the control of Sheriff's office held by the ordinary suffrages. Criminals or troublemakers found it difficult to hide behind an office that was accountable to the people. Like it was possible in the medieval ages when such a thing was possible. The two local offices, the Mayor and the Sherriff's after the advent of democratic process in Europe, were mainly responsible for the progress of its society. The peace and tranquillity that this process brought among the people and the restoration of faith in the administration, which no longer was repressive and bowed to the popular thought, brought much change.

The countries or nations, which brought about these changes earlier then their neighbours developed with greater speed. Faster than those who copied these systems after getting to know the benefits that this system had provided to their powerful and developed neighbouring nations. The fear of defeat by the armies of strong nations brought about these changes. The nation that had better administrative system and hence a strong military and a content subject population was powerful and ready to subjugate others.

The Judicial system too was much localised after the advent of democracy in European Nations and it too contributed for the evolution of the Western Society. However, this system spread rather quite quickly, first in the Western Europe and then into the Central Part and eventually it reached most of the Eastern European Nations too.

When the Europeans had a new world to turn to and populate, this system carried into the Americas and the Latin countries. Moreover, this system was the hallmark of the Western Civilization and the cause of its prosperity and power. American system of administration is by fa the best. It is much decentralized and hence progressive. The only thing that hinders the pace of development in America is its racial divide. If America had a single ethnic population, it would have raced past all nations very quickly due to its decentralized system. The Caucasian population want their society governed by a certain rules that the Black community not evolved to understand. The Caucasian population on the hand not evolved to think what is best for the minorities that belong to other races. This misunderstanding has and is causing much trouble for the lawmakers and the law enforcers of the USA. It is also the cause of mistrust between both the races. Its ethnic divide is the only thing that keeps its society troubled and once that problem somehow solved, the USA shall be the far ahead in all human innovations.

All Western as well as Non-Western Nations that fill the slot of developed nations recognises the importance and efficiency of this system. In addition, they recognise its role in the developmental process. Hence, these nations have advocated a non-centralized system in the spheres of civil administration, policing, and justice delivery. The Western Society in the long course of its history and the lessons learnt by it, through the trails and errors of time, changed itself in a controlled manner. It in a phased pattern rid itself of the obsolete centralised administrative system. That was in fact practised by the Kingdoms and Empires of the by gone years. The Western society opted for a decentralised system of running its nations for the betterment of its culture and protection of its borders. The Eastern nations have not understood the value of this system for progress into the future.

On the contrary, in all the Authoritarian and Eastern Nations, the administrative systems are much centralised. The officials are immune to prosecution even if they misuse their official positions or make it a cue for amassing wealth through corrupt methods and nepotism. Their authority is under the control of a central authority that is inaccessible to the ordinary people. In addition, elected governments auction official positions to the highest bidder, selected for collection of money for oneself and for the corrupt central authorities. Just like, it happened in the kingdoms of the past. Hence, the Authoritarian and Eastern Nations have not recognised the importance of these offices in the development of their society and for making their societies at par with the Western Nations.

The Eastern Nations, even those that are democracies, run their countries like empires and kingdoms. Even though time has not favoured such establishments and neither can this central system benefit the people in any way? This system is, in fact, very cruel in supressing the aspirations of the general population. This one big fault is the greatest dead weight that slows the progress of the Eastern Nations. This drawback prevents them from joining the list of developed nations. It is very Eastern to be authoritarian. It is very Eastern to be repressive and to rise above the rest of fellow men through every mean possible. Without caring for the surroundings in which ones children shall grow and propagate.

However, this central system of administration has destroyed morality from within the Eastern Societies. It has made them corrupt and decadent. These Centralized systems are in clash with local customs that evolved along with the evolution of these societies. Those local customs and traditions that have checked corruption in the Eastern Societies have generally been supressed by the centralized administrative systems. Making the Eastern nations regress in evolution and progress. This repression shall remain with the Eastern nations because of their genetic makeup. It cannot change at any cost. However, this system accounts for much discontentment among the general population and is very dangerous in the modern world. The Eastern societies shall remain slaves just as their ancestors or these societies shall rise up like the people of early modern Europe and destroy all who stand in the way of their freedom and prosperity.

Western nations have excelled in other social areas too, in which the Eastern Society has failed miserably. They are laws formulated for the betterment of a society so that it functions as a healthy body, without ailment. At times when obsolete laws became a hindrance for proper functioning of a society these are changed. The societies that became stagnant during the medieval ages, that is, all Eastern Societies. These were living in the same social framework for centuries. Their laws and customs did not change once these embedded deep into the cultures. In addition, these stagnant laws and customs made these societies stagnant and backward compared to the Western Culture. The Western society changed a bit every half a century and took it out of the dark ages and out of the authoritarian system, to become a new system capable of change, for the advancement of its people.

However, for formulating new laws and changing the old ones a very farsighted vision and legislation had to develop within the Western Societies. That vision and will provided by the civil unrest prevalent among the European People during the start of the modern age brought about by the spread of education within the common masses. For their own protection and for the appeasement of the people the ruling class had to bow to popular demands and gave in in to successive legislation that made the people more free and integrated such laws into the system of their nation's administration. Nevertheless, these laws formulated and changed at times. The Western Culture has taken no chances in implementing those laws and rule through those laws that have made their nations worthwhile in living conditions.

The lessons that the Western World has learnt during the past, especially during the days of the 'Black Death' and the revolutionary times of early and late modern age has made these nations adhere to these laws with a strict view. Hence, their cities are far cleaner, their health system is quite advanced, and their pollution levels are decreasing constantly. Their civic establishments are working in comparatively good health. All this is possible because of the involvement of the common people in the upkeep of their laws. Laws devised for the betterment of their civil society. Moreover, the government's working is transparent and questionable by the citizens. The Western World appreciates the role of private enterprise in economic development. Because it relates to the volatiles of the markets, of supply and demand and the purpose of providing, much needed taxes for civic development and maintenance. Nevertheless, private enterprise has kept under the regulatory control of the government.

On the contrary, the Eastern Governments have much disregard for laws. The centralised systems keep the people away from any decision-making and functional part of their nation. It is easy for the rulers of these systems to break free from the constraints of law. They enforce their will and the will of their lobbies on the hapless and helpless society. The armed constabularies and security forces are effectively used to supress all forms of discontent against the rulers. They serve as tool of state repression in these Eastern authoritarian type nations. With no checks and balances on the misadventures of these rulers are in place, as long as they have possession over political power.

Due to these wide spread malfunctions in the Eastern Nations, their cities are in dilapidated conditions with no civic amenities available for the citizens. The waters are polluted and full of disease. Infrastructure has reached its end with no revenue for its upkeep. There is no effective enforcement of law. Law-enforcing agencies turn their guns on the people. They have no training to control traffic on the roads. The majority of law enforcers generate wealth through illegitimate and criminal activities and employ cruel methods of suppression to keep the discontent population under control through the element of fear. The regulatory bodies themselves provide for the businesses to indulge in unfair methods as long as these businesses provide for the upkeep of the families of officials who run the offices of these regulatory bodies. Hence, these bodies let the businesses run with immunity regarding flouting of norms laid down to protect the people and their surroundings.

Every evil practised in the Eastern Nations is due to this major flaw. This fault is taking the social standing of the Eastern world towards an abyss. Adulteration in food and pharmaceuticals, unfair trade practices, release of industrial effluents into the environment without wastewater management and unchecked tax evasion are rampant in the Eastern nations. These malpractices have destroyed the health of the people, polluted the environment, and made the economies of the Eastern nations unhealthy and beyond the capacity of recovery.

In the countries that were once colonies of the European Nations, the European administrators enforced every law and regulation to make the society free from evils and ran efficiently. Nevertheless, even half a century of self-rule in these colonies, has destroyed every institution that was responsible for the upkeep and enforcement of laws and regulations. Those same laws adopted from the colonial rulebooks to suit the local needs, which worked efficiently during the colonial times. This shows the degradation of the Eastern Mind and its contempt for an orderly society. A society that provides for all its population on equal terms is not suited for the Eastern population.

Due to this, the hardworking and laborious people, who have the potential to raise in the society through their enterprise, business management skills and articulate trade practices usually do not make it to the upper rungs of the society in the modern Eastern Nations. Nevertheless, people who make wealth through illegitimate and corrupt methods rise in these societies and further the deterioration of the Eastern World. Hence, the Eastern Nations have not yet recognised the importance of laws and regulations and their enforcement. Laws and regulations are very important for social development and progress of their nations.

Because ordinary citizens have no say in the administration of their nations, they are at the receiving end of corrupt officials. They have powers beyond the means of ordinary population's protests. Like the officials of the crown, during the medieval ages in Europe. That medieval psyche has still not drained out of the Eastern

Bureaucrat, even after centuries have passed when such practices prevailed in the Western World. Maybe due to the powers invested in the political and bureaucratic offices in the Eastern Nations, all who assume power are against its distribution among the people. They rather indulge in misuse of these powers without remorse. In addition, most people who have desire to join the civil services in all Eastern Countries are willing to go to great extents for government employment. Moreover, they are willingly pay huge bribes to join powerful offices, both bureaucratic and military.

This Eastern practise has witnessed large-scale immigration of able and educated people from Eastern Nations to enter the Western Economies. Through their abilities, these immigrants contribute towards the Western world's evolvement. These same people could have contributed in their own countries and would have proven as assets of great value for taking the Eastern People out of their rotten systems. They would have prepared it to compete with the other half of world that is developed. This brain drain especially after the 1960 AD has cost the Eastern Economies dear. No concrete steps taken by the decision makers to create equal opportunities for these people in the East. The decision makers of the Eastern Countries do not want to let go off the iron grasp they have over their populations and economies of the nations that they rule. Hence are not willing to create a system of equal opportunities.

The past and present times have provided enough evidence that under no circumstances shall the Eastern World rid itself of these flaws. Because have the Eastern Populations never revolted against an oppressor, be it either an individual or an organisation. In addition, it shall probably never attain the vital courage that is necessary for the ordinary and common people to bring about changes for the betterment of their future generations. Like the changes brought about in the Western World by its common people. Whose descendants are reaping the fruits of their ancestors' attempts at changing the world?

The Western nations developed when their borders contained people who spoke one language and practised the same religion. Their culture too was the same. When democracy came to these lands through years of struggle these people, saw them as one. A strong sense of cohesion developed that held the society of these nations together. This cohesion gave birth to nationalism, the other reason for the greatness of the Western nations. The Eastern countries have borders created ages ago by the armies with force. Either Eastern Armies or European Armies had annexed lands that were linguistically and ethnically much different. However, due to certain circumstances these different people could not create their own nations even after the demise of colonialism due to their backwardness and lack of military power. The addition of these different stocks of people by force into one nation is not nation building but occupation and hegemony. As these ethnicities are in danger of being discriminated against. Attempts made by the rulers to change the demography of the areas that these subjugated ethnicities inhabit also prevail. Moreover, such activities breed armed struggles, making these nations at war within their own borders and with its own people. As we have seen during the nineteenth century much disorderly internal strives have consumed many Eastern Nations and dried up their resources. The resources those are necessary for development. These factors do not let many Eastern Nations develop on the lines of European Nations of the 18th Century when nationalism was coming into being. If these Eastern Nations do not let the individual ethnic stocks to develop independently, such nationalistic feelings shall never be part of the Eastern World. The artificially drawn borders of the Eastern nations shall fall due to mismanagement of its society.

The real progress of the Eastern World shall commence when all ethnicities and linguistic societies, given the chance to administer their own people on the lines of the European Countries make this society a success. The European nations in spite of being small and compact have given more to the world in progressing from an ancient tribe to a modern world. The European Nations have taken much less in return. However, for these small principalities to exist in The Eastern World or the Third World is near to impossible. As no one in the Eastern World shall want to give up the lands annexed at the expense of others.

All past history and modern life has provided for the world to see that while Western Society has provided all the technology and lifestyle factors that are predominant in the world. The Eastern World has not been able to evolve accordingly, even after receiving innovations from the West in the form of governance. The Eastern Nations cannot develop according to the principles of the Western World because of the evolutionary process that directs all people to follow their instincts. Moreover, that instinct itself provides enough difference between the East and the West. Even in the evolutionary process, the east is much less in social development.

It has been less than 100 years since all the Eastern Populations have been exposed to a daily life which is predominately Western and filled with Western Innovations and Mechanisations. All that has evolved through the trails of errors of the Western Society, it has provided to east. The Eastern People have been exposed these lifestyles and the laws by their colonial rulers or governments keen on developing their colonies on the lines of the Western World. It has been done mainly to match its military might without coming to understand that for the longer period of its existence the Eastern Society and its people have not been given the right ingredients to match the lifestyle that has so suddenly been placed in their midst. Hence, Westernisation of most nations in Africa and Asia has failed. Alternatively, it is bound to fail in the future. Without doubt, because the people of these nations have not yet understood the principle of this system. Even at present times, it is very alien and very complex for them to come to terms with this political evolution. In addition, this is the reason that the governments in most Eastern nations are finding it difficult to come to understand the mess that they have created for themselves.

Hence, it is quite difficult for the Eastern World that has already lost much and vital time in not being able to compete with the Western World due to its societal weaknesses, customs, and its helplessness in strengthening its culture. It is beyond the control of the Eastern People to think on the lines of Western nations due to the biochemical make up of their bodies. Maybe the course of evolution for the Eastern People is markedly different from the evolution of the Western People. The mutations that the European Lands and Environments induced in the people of the West are taking the people of the West towards a completely different route of social evolution. That shall most probably be responsible for the extinction of the Eastern Society if it shall not recognise its flaws.

The Eastern Civilization that resides in the nations of Africa and Asia and their populations are living with the ghosts of the past. In a belief when they were great nations but have at present do not even give their half-hearted efforts to reach the greatness that they believe once existed in some distant past. Moreover, their present doings belies their claim on any great contribution to the people, who have survived the past to live in the present. Except the Japanese and the Chinese Leadership, who awakened themselves from this Eastern Slumber, a sleep that creates dreams full of ignorance and superstitions?

The only sincere efforts to compete with the Western World by getting rid of its obsolete customs, that has prevented the growth of all Eastern Nations been undertaken by the Japanese, who have succeeded. The Chinese too come in this category of people, who are still trying but maybe the route that they took, Communism, has delayed their development. However, this has not eliminated their chances of competing with the Western Nations. The Chinese are trying to understand the values of other systems of governance and correcting their future by amending their past mistakes.

The leadership of these nations are truly wise for they have realised that if their societies do not change then they shall head for a complete extinction of their race and their culture. That extinction shall come at the hands of the ever-evolving culture that has spread out of Western Europe into the new world and shall finally engulf the world, one day. Nevertheless, for reasons unknown, the other nations of Eastern Part of the world have never developed the insight that the Japanese and the Chinese Leaders had developed. In addition, they are not willing to make certain essential changes either by force or through policy to protect their progeny. Maybe they are doing so because these leaders after the fall of the Eastern World have intentions to settle in the Western World along with their families and live a life of ease and comfort. The wealth amassed through corruption and nepotism at the expense of their brethren who suffer endless miseries shall provide for their progeny in the Western world.

If the Western World evolves in isolation, like during the medieval period, when the Europeans did not enter the North African and Asian Realms. When Christianity and Islam were hated enemies of each other and there was very little exchange of ideas between the East and the West. The evolution of the Eastern World shall cease. In addition, it shall come to a halt, at some places the evolution shall regress and flow back. Moreover, the Eastern World devoid of ideas shall function as a place consumed in a flame of ignorance. However, why the people of the East or their leaders have not realised this, too is a matter of concern?

The Future that Waits

The 21st Century shall bring many new changes in the world. Changes of welcome for some and changes of hopelessness for others wait in the future. The reasons for both happiness and gloom, being the forms of governments and the methods of governance practised. The present human societies, according to the geographical distribution of humans on the planet, have divided into various races, religions, and political systems. The division of humans according to the way they carry out their daily political activities is the most important. Politics is the activity that regulates every other social practise of human civilization.

The Western World grouped into a bloc in which all of Europe, North America are included is one sphere of human division. Also included in it are Israel, Australia, and New Zealand, as these too are together in this realm. The Developed Countries include the Western World, Japan, and Russia. However, the Russian Federation, the way its government being at present, is not part of the Western World, it can be but in half. The people of Japan are very different in relation to other Mongoloid People. The Japanese are a mixture of different human races Mongloid and Non Mongoloid, like the Northern Ainu, who still have some Non-Mongloid remnants quite visible on their bodies. Nevertheless, these mixtures, favoured by the climatic conditions of the Japanese islands have induced the people of Japan with much positive virtues of progress. This environment has bred into these same people a sense of social responsibility and discipline rarely found among the people of Asia.

Latin America is another geographical region that is distinct from other parts of the globe. All Latin American Countries share a common link in language, social structure, and political environment. The Semi Developed Countries, which include China and Most of the South East Asia, form another bloc in the present world polity. The Middle East, which includes North Africa, Western Asia, and Central Asia, which united by Islam as a unifying character among the populations of these countries and their culture is another political sphere of human political division. Sub Saharan Africa is another section of society, the population being Negroid, sharing many common forms of social institution and largely common political practices. South Asia is another part of the world that divides from the rest of the world because of its common forms of governments and social Institutions, largely derived from a common history. The human future judged from the present conditions of these various blocs that the world division portrays, due to present circumstances and world politics is easy if observed discernibly.

The Western World is a large democratic institution. The barriers of language, the only character that divides it, separate it. However, the west united by a common religion, a very similar way of life and largely common interest of its peoples and their representatives. These countries share a common democratic form of government, which is very essential for the survival of its society and its relative prosperity. This society is uniting. The unification of Europe shall be first step towards its new order of things. The formation of NATO has already started the unification process militarily, for the protection of this society. This carried forward by formation of the European Union. These countries much advanced in infrastructure layout, scientific research, technological advancements, economic policies, and general social welfare for its citizens. The real cause of progress in these fields is the form of government practiced in these countries. The governments in these countries work for creating employment opportunities in their countries. So that the public remains, busy in nation building. These systems provide a spirit of honest labour and enterprise and try to follow the free market enterprise system, creating equal opportunities for all. Human freedom is at its epitome in these democracies. This system provides a governmental system that is not altogether centralised and provide for local governance even in the realm of law and order.

Maintenance of law and order, the enforcement of laws and upkeep of justice are the pillars on which any society rests. These are the most important things that repose a citizen's trust in one's nation and makes a citizen feel protected within the borders of one's country. The nations who have invested the heaviest in these principles are the ones who have become powerful nations, with a good economy. A country at peace within its borders and can become a powerful military giant. The Western Nations have no doubt invested the heaviest in these principles of human society for their development.

Democracies in these nations have given equal opportunity for people to rise at the highest levels in social sphere. All have the opportunity to rise to the highest political office if they are holders of a genuine character and supported by the people. In these nations, an individual is important than the state and the state exists because of its citizens. There is no single master of the nation and there is no guarantee if any individual shall hold the highest office for life. Hence, no one adopts such policies that are against the peaceful existence of the people. Lest the people bring in effect a change of their leader, the one who does not maintain the decorum of one's office.

Due to minimal government interference in daily lives of the people, these societies are developing towards growth at a pace unthought-of by other parts of the world. These political systems have an inbuilt mechanism to provide for welfare needs of the society. The people do not feel oppressed by the system. These political orders have devised ways to stop monopolistic dreams of any manipulating individual or company.

At present, the Western World is much dependent upon the Middle East for its energy supplies, in the form of crude oil and its derivatives. Ever since the discovery of mineral oil in the North African, Sub Saharan, and Asian Fields, the dependence of the Western World for this resource has ever increased. This resource has also been a major source of trouble for the Western World. To secure an assured supply of oil from these Third World Countries, the Western Countries have interfered in the internal affairs of the Third World Countries. They have also supported and protected governments who can assure the Western world a supply of oil that is cheap, irrespective of the aspirations of the local populations. This is the major reason of discontent against the Western World in the Muslim Realm. This feeling of hatred fostered by relationship that mineral oil has created. Oil is the cause that is causing tensions of great magnitude between the West and the Middle East. This has turned the each other enemies. Both the worlds are willing to go to great extents to keep the flame of enmity burning. As long as the flame in the refineries of the Middle East lights for the Western World the flame of this enmity shall remain lit.

The game changer in this field shall come up in the Western World by 2050 AD. When in a race to solve its energy problems the Western Word by this period shall be in a position to build small-scale nuclear reactors. They will be much smaller than their present monstrous build. The small size of these nuclear reactors shall render them much safe and for safety of the population. The reactors, to protect the population in case of any eventuality, placed under the ground these reactors shall pose negligible danger. These nuclear reactors shall be a replacement for carbon fuel based turbines. The fuel used at present for the production of electricity. The West and the Developed countries shall phase out coal-based power plants. No coal power plants that dot the surface of the Western or Developed Countries will exist. The Western economy shall lose its dependence on the carbon-based fuel to light up its cities and energize its industrial production facilities except those fuels derived from biomass. With this new technology to make electricity, a huge exercise to lay vast network of rails to accommodate transportation for both the individuals and the materials shall commence. The energy production shall favour mass transport and logistics use in every possible method to recover full economic advantages.

This period shall also witness airborne travel systems both for individual and mass transport within the cities. Just like modern automobiles, but with propellers to make them rise and move in the air. All this made possible by the efficient chemical reactors that shall power these airborne locomotives. By 2045 AD, the Western Economy shall have assembled small chemical reactors in the form of fuel cells. These reactors will be efficient in energy storage and conversion into mechanical form of energy to power the engines of its vehicles, marine vessels, and airplanes. With such technological inventions coming up and spreading in the Western World by 2050 AD its dependence of the natural carbon based fuels shall be totally reduced. With no requirement for mineral fuel, the Western world shall not interfere in affairs of the Middle East and the Muslim World.

Mining for carbon-based fuels shall virtually come to a halt in the Western World. Mining or drilling carried out, shall most probably be for the manufacture of plastics or chemicals for other processes. This surplus of energy in the Western World shall usher in a period of hectic scientific activity. For now, the investment in research shall be in the scientific area of human endeavour, due to reduction in the cost of energy production. The dependence on fuels for transportation and logistics supply no longer on foreign shores, the Western Democratic Nations shall enjoy great independence for making progress that the human society has never witnessed.

By 2045 AD, pharmacological interventions in medicine shall end and genetic interventions shall take their place. New inventions in the field of medicine and biotechnology shall unite the two very inexplicably. Biotechnology shall eventually transform the practice of medicine into more result-based science. Medicine will be less dependent on chemical interventions and shall rely upon the human body's own internal molecules for curing its diseases. The advent of biotechnology shall be visible in agriculture too. A surplus of energy shall make it possible to irrigate once barren lands with genetically modified plants to suit the most arid of regions. Soilless agriculture 'factories' shall provide abundant of food for the populations of the Western World by 2045 AD.

The surplus energy shall also be responsible for setting up large production facilities. These shall make use of the science of artificial intelligence and robotics to create workforce out of robots. Hence, these production facilities will make industrial production cheap and without labour problems. Human intervention in manufacturing facilities shall remain limited to the controls of the robotic workers through computer programs and artificial intelligence networks. Cost of production will go down with these innovations. The industrial products of the Western World shall be in a position to outcompete the other economies of the world. This will generate surplus revenue in the World Economy for the Western and The Developed World.

The Third World Economies by this time will have depleted their natural resources for energy generation. Even if they do not deplete their resources, most countries of the Third World shall have ill-managed economies for maintenance of their old power generation facilities. During these years the Eastern Economies, barring a few, like Japan, China and few countries in South East Asia, will not have the revenue or resources to plan, build and maintain the new technological innovations for energy generation. Hence, they shall be much deficient in industrial production due to the deficit in power industry.

Waste management technology of the Western World shall keep its cities and towns clean, and pollution free. Energy generation and much metal and mineral wealth shall be recycled through the recovery from waste of the human settlements. Such influx of prosperity into the Western Economy shall make it a breeding ground for scientific research. Social evolution shall speed up comparable to as it was during the 1800 AD, when rest of the world was still in the dark ages.

By 2060 AD, the Western World should have a complete protection from the danger of a nuclear threat, with a missile shield set up in the interstellar space just above the Earth. This missile shield shall have the capability to destroy inter-continental ballistic missiles at the site of their launch. This disruption done by manipulating the electronic circuit in the warhead carrier through satellites armed with impulse devices. With this threat gone, the Western World shall have a great pressure removed from its mind. To secure its citizens further from the dangers of war. A large network of underground tunnels constructed to serve the dual purpose of public transport and to serve as shelters against a nuclear threat will proceed continuously.

Hence, by 2055 AD, with dependence on natural fuels removed. Medicine and agriculture practices shall fully support the Western population's health and hunger. With human drudgery reduced to the minimal and the threat of destruction nearly removed by 2060 AD. The Western part of human society shall be very different from the rest of the world.

With progress, the military prowess of Western Democracies shall increase manifold. No nation on Earth shall be in a position to match the military power of the Western World by 2070 AD. The Western World shall be a dominant force on the World for a long time to come after the 2070 AD. According to records of the past, this civilization shall any time after this timeline or in the 22nd Century be the first humans to settle on some distant planet or at least build a colony on the moon. Because their inner self shall not let this human society settle in contentment. In accordance with its past exploits, this human race's nature will force it to seek new ways to explore the distant lands. Even if these lands known in the future to exist on far away planets separated by the seas of rare gases called the 'space'. But the reason for all this development is and will be very basic, democracy, decentralized local governance, equal opportunities for all and respect for individual freedom and dignity. All this change from the present way of life shall surely happen in the entire developed world as a whole, North America, Europe, Japan, Australia and New Zealand shall reap the full harvest of this coming change.

Decentralisation of the political system of the Russian Federation is necessary for it become a Westernised nation. If its political leaders mend their ways and pave way for a fairer and less repressive democratic system, Russia will also be a part of this world and reap its success. Else, it shall stand midway like the Czarist state of the past. It will be neither too modern to be part of the west nor too backward to be counted among the Eastern Semi Developed Economies. However, since the Eastern Part of Europe has much mixture of Caucasian blood with the Middle Eastern and the Mongloid People, the form of government in these regions, especially Russia has very little chance of becoming a total democracy. Its political authority shall always remain in the hands of autocratic elite. They shall be unwilling to give the people complete freedom to choose their fate. State repression might remain the same and centralized form of government, which has always been present in Russia under the Tsars, the Bolsheviks and even still under their form of democracy, will always hand over powers of huge magnitude to its rulers. To use it to control any political unrest directed against the political offices of those in political power.

Russia is a classic case of travelling in two boats, caught between the East and the West. The population of Russian Federation has a population much mixed in blood. It is having both the East and the West running inside its veins. Its political system too is trying to making shifts between the two corners. However, not finding balance on this scale. Hence, it is rocking in this confusion as to which system is better for its population, the Eastern Authoritarian or the Western Democratic. Even at present, it is an issue hotly debated issue in the power circles of Russian Federation.

Latin America, culturally, is part of the Western World. but politically and economically it is not part of the Western civilization., hence it is a separate part in the political world division quite apart from its parent Latin culture from which it derives its name. The Latin American System of governance is in part democratic but controlled by the Crony Capitalists and Autocrats. Every new government elected or enforced upon the people of Latin America is quite repressive and showers favours upon the highest bidder. The Latin American Governments favour the rich and let the rich exploit the poor so that they may never rise above the line of poverty. This is visible in the ghettos that have surrounded all major Latin American Cities and Metropolitan settlements.

Hence, Latin America has never been a place equated with the Western World in living standards and social equality, the two qualities that make a nation great. Nevertheless, for that maybe some racial reasons are also be involved. Its culture is very much Western but without the spark that will carry the Western World through the present times into the age of a bright future. Because the population of Southern America is mixed and while the European conquerors' blood might want to evolve into the free market democratic society, other genetic components of their blood might have a shift towards a governmental system that has an iron grip over its people. This system enforces the policies of each new government to run a nation. However, this political division has not favoured laws that have evolved through the years for a culture to expand and grow. Widespread misuse of government offices and political positions will never make Latin America rise in the world economy until there is some drastic change in this system. This change brought about by human intervention or by the wrath of nature, it will never come by itself.

By 2050 AD, the population of many Latin American Countries will suffer the effects of Industrial effluents and unhygienic living conditions in the cities. Not supported by an efficient medical network the population shall be diseased by many viral communicable afflictions brought upon by pollutants and human waste. Sensing the present conditions in the city and towns of the Latin American Nations, the conditions are quite depressing in accordance with living standards required for humans. These miserable conditions in the future shall be present themselves more aggressively in the Southern Part of the continent and shall be less severe in the Northern Part. There is a chance that disease shall wreak havoc and the local authorities shall not be in a position to control the epidemic. Depopulation of Vast areas of land by the pathetic living conditions of the urban poor will definitely happen. The urban poor shall spread the disease to the rural areas through communication and shall bring the population of the Latin America down in great numbers.

Due to such conditions, immigrations from Europe and North America shall bring a lot of Western World into the South American Continent and by 2050 AD. This immigration shall be on the same lines as European immigrants arrived in the United States during the 1930s and 1940s. However, the immigrants coming in Latin America shall mostly be from the North American continent and Europe too shall contribute its share in human capital that will arrive in the Latin America. Maybe, after these immigrations fill the void left after depopulation of whole areas, Latin America shall no longer remain Latin but be a collection of different ethnicities. Then, South America will be a melting pot that shall melt within it more than the melting pot of North American has melted inside it.

This shall be the real Westernisation of the Latin America. Although Latin America has the language of Western Europe, the culture of Western Europe and the same religion it could not shine with the same glitter. It does not possess the qualities of the continent, which provided Latin America its present identity. Since most of the people who changed Latin America culturally and racially, after Christopher Columbus entered its exterior boundaries, came from the South Western parts of Europe. These parent nations have not had that level of development in European as other nations of its upper Western parts. The countries that provided Latin America with its human resource still lag behind the countries from which the North American population immigrated. This could be the reason that Authoritarian regimes survive and sustain like a vermin under a stone. In addition, just one weak moment is enough for this parasite to infest the nations of Latin America with the contents of its disease.

The South American Continent with its changed population will have changed political policies and by 2060 AD. The Latin American Countries shall be part of Western Civilization, with all its amenities and privileges due to these drastic changes. The Latin American Countries will equal the Western World with economies comparable to any other developed country after 2070 AD. This is something that at present is not possible in the continent of South America.

Parts of Russia, China, and South East Asia are part of the world circle circled as semi-developed. Russia is part of the Western World in its culture but its present form of Autocratic and Authoritarian Government cannot take it to that level of human development. Its political system cannot make the society evolve comparable to a Western Democracy. The countries of the Mongoloid World except Japan, countries like China, The Koreas, and all nations demarcated on the map of South East Asia come under the category of the Semi Developed World. Some although are part of the Third World in some measures. Although these countries have done well compared to the nations of the Middle East, South Asia, and Africa and cannot be part of their bloc. They still do not possess the spirit to attain the same level of sophistication and development that is inherent in the Western World and Japan.

However, if the Japanese people could make changes in their thinking and their social behaviours to compete with the Western World, why the other nations in its vicinity could not, is very distressing. The educated and the enlightened Chinese, through revolution changed the administration of China but have done it with pace. They tried to follow the Japanese pattern of social change but by choosing the communist culture. However, they could not make the same changes and with it the quickness, like the Japanese could.

Communism is a good prospect when presented on paper. The communist ideology and the writers who are its proponents have given the society the idea of equality in distribution of the wealth of this world. However, in writing all the treatises on the communist theory and how it should be practised, the Fathers of Communism had overlooked one human character which is the cause and the reason that communism can never be put into practice the way it is put into the books. That human drawback is greed. As long as greed is, an integral part of the human character

Communism is impossible. Until greed easily presents itself in the people who make decisions about the allotment of resources, communism is impossible. This is an important aspect of society overlooked by the communist theory. No one on this world is altruistic enough to benefit one's fellow beings in relation to one's family, ones near ones and one's personal self. It is very important as to who is responsible for providing equal share in the population of a nation or a society. In whose hands can this responsibility handed in without misuse, does that person exist on this planet? Through times the ones who became decision makers of a communist society or nation, are the ones who abused their powers the most and indulged in luxuries while the people suffered.

If the Chinese had followed some other pattern of change and not the communist pattern, it would have been better for the Chinese people. China would have reached the same heights that Japan has reached in spheres of technology and infrastructure development. Maybe China could develop to heights much greater than Japan. If it had followed, the Japanese Model of change but that is something that never happened and might never happen in the near future.

The Semi Developed World has a political system, which gives some form of opportunities in trade and commerce to the common people. In fact, the governments of these systems promote these activities in order to generate revenue. Nevertheless, the established order of political system in these countries is very rigid and does not advocate change. The political systems of these countries are very centralized and oppressive. This political system is effective in crushing the aspirations of the people. It gives unprecedented powers to the bureaucracy and the political leadership. These systems shall never allow the common people political freedom. It shall crush any movement that want such a change, due which the common people shall never become participants in political system of these nations.

The political organisations in these countries advocate freedom of trade and commerce to keep their populations busy in revenue generation. While the political offices live off the sweat and blood of the people. Official corruption will always remain in these systems, no matter what. It is a mean for the government-controlled sectors to amass wealth and store these illegitimate revenue gains in the vaults of major tax havens. Most of which will always remain within the Western Economies' Borders. The political leaders of these countries are aware of the fact that their luxuries are part of a healthy inflow of revenue. Hence, they want such policies that are no hindrance to new investments and for creation of business opportunities. Such countries shall keep the steady pace of development going for many years. However, these nations will remain recipients of second hand innovations from the Western World. These countries will never rise up to the level of developed countries even in the near future.

The Middle East has never known peace. All armies that came from North Africa into Asia desecrated its peace. All cohorts that marched with their arms out of Europe to trample these lands made calmness escape its people. Moreover, all the nomadic horses that beat the sands of the Middle East under their hoofs made it a battlefield. None of them has ever let tranquillity to remain the Middle East. Peace is never going to stay in the Middle East even for centuries to come. The people of the Middle East will ever suffer the harshness of war and conflict, that shall come from all sides and from within it. Because of its multitude ethnic hatred, the hate that is bred deep into the souls of the people of the Middle East.

The Middle East has a political setup in which its armies and constabularies are a tool of suppression against its own people. Although mineral carbon based fuels' mining has given this geographical location much political importance at present. This same mineral wealth has turned it into a warzone due to its mineral wealth.

In the Middle Eastern political systems, the political leaders and government officials have a tendency to be very ruthless in combating all expressions of freedom and are usually very corrupt. In these systems the people in control, reap the rewards of all the national wealth that time and geology has showered upon their lands. These political leaders want to keep the general masses poor. In addition, they believe that if kept under-developed and improvised, it shall be easy to control the population with guns and cannons.

The bane of the Middle East is that its population for centuries altogether, had rulers who have tried to take authority either from God in the form of 'Priest Kings' or later through the name of Prophet Mohammed. They have done it just for the sake of ruling. They have crushed the aspirations of the people in doing so. As rulers of the past crushed the people of the Middle East under their heavy rule, be it the Romans, the Persians, the Caliphs, or the Sultans.

The Middle East has rarely known peace and it most likely that tranquillity shall not conquer it. It shall not calm down either through the fear of destructive wars or through the lure of serenity brought by harmony. It a point where many cultures meet, a centre stage for North Africa, Europe, and Central Asia to vent out their anger. Moreover, this never let its sands become the oasis that can provide respite and shade for the sweltering nations of the Middle East.

Although Islam advocates personal freedom and on the shoulders of personal freedom and purity in public dealings it conquered the entire world. Nevertheless, the land that gave Islam to the world has not been able to come to terms with personal freedom. Moreover, all form of political activity in the Middle East tries to be repressive. As this land fragments between tribal loyalties and the age-old practice of the misuse of political authority, widely present in all the Middle Eastern Nations.

The political environment of the Middle East seems to favour authoritarian governments strongly. This is a quality deeply embedded in its sands. It is flowing deep within veins of the people of the Middle East, that is, the majority of them. The people have a strong inclination towards oppressive rulers. They favour an authoritarian ruling class or else the lands of the Middle East would never have such governments in the first place.

However, the authoritarian governments no matter where ever they exist do not let the society evolve and to progress. It sticks the society to some ideas and blindly follows those ideas until a new authoritarian regime overthrows the old system and enforces new ideologies on the people. That is exactly happening in the Middle East.

However, the authoritarian governments favour the interests of the few. These governments are for those who rule and their dependents. While this political system largely ignores the aspirations, demands and needs of the majority of the population. Moreover, eventually leads the society into degeneration and decay, with no scope of progress in to the future. For these reasons, the Middle East shall never be able to compete with the Western World in the coming days of the future. It will be an easy target for military hardware dealers and warmongers, who will bring misfortune for the people of the Middle East in the near future.

After the mineral wealth of the Middle East is of no use for powering the automobiles and heating the homes in the Western World the wars in it shall increase. It shall no longer have protection of the nations that benefit from its mineral wealth and try much to stop it from becoming a warzone. The people of the Middle Eastern nations are very easily motivated to play into the hands of the powers beyond its sands, those who have always used one tribe against the other but the people of the Middle East still, even in this century love playing this game. However, with the advent of small sized nuclear reactors and chemical reactors, the dependence of Western World on mineral fuel shall end and this region shall lose its importance by 2050 AD.

The Middle East is a vortex. It made so by the mineral wealth that it stands over and the people who want to sell it for making fortunes, also by the nations who want to buy it and have the technology to extract it for their economies. Nevertheless, it will not remain like this forever.

The Middle East, by 2050 AD, shall go down into a hole of ignorance and poverty. There will be much lawlessness in this part of the world. Warlords will control small stretches of land and there shall be much infighting among the populations for control of whatever left for them to use for their benefit. Scientific innovations and technological novelties shall never reach its borders. Its population shall at large remain illiterate. Moreover, the region shall become a market of small and medium arms for the Western World's weapons factories. The Western World shall only interfere in these countries to sell their war wares and keep the infighting among the populations of the Middle East going on.

The Middle Eastern Countries shall remain imbedded in poverty and their economies shall remain sickly. The population of these countries shall remain under the constant threat of civil war and changing regimes. However, all this shall happen when its mineral wealth is no longer gold for the Western World. This shall happen after 2050 AD.

The Middle East shall revert to the tribal society it once was during the middle ages. One tribe will fight the other for supremacy in this age. The region will never rid itself of dictatorial governments. Those governments who will rule on sectarian lines shall line very corner and hillock of this area. This will never let the people of the Middle East unite under a strong democracy. Hence, it will never march towards progress.

The Sub Saharan Africa is a world in turmoil. It is still living in a tribal setup. The idea of a nation with many tribes in collaborative nation building is, even, at this time alien to the Sub Saharan African Communities. Even at places that were once part of the British Empire or were colonies of the French or Belgians, the well laid infrastructure and organised system of government has deteriorated. All this has happened because the Real Africa still wants to live in shantytowns and small settlements. Africa under the colonial rule was at peace with itself. The colonial rulers did not allow the disputes between different tribes to flare up. After the Colonial Powers left Africa, it slowly started to become true to its name and slipped back into the 'Dark Continent, it was once. The people of Africa, despite of being subject to the worst atrocities that any human population has ever faced, have not understood the meaning of freedom.

Instead of building nations, the Sub Saharan African Leaders have concentrated on particular tribes for remaining in power and for filling their coffers with money looted from their own nations. These leaders want to abandon the nations once ousted from power and live in some Western land. Few African leaders have the intellect to save their continent and its people from the ignorance and division. Many such leaders have paid dearly for their vision regarding the future of their home. If Africa can produce more of such sons on the map of its existence and make them reach out to their people, they might save Africa, but who knows?

The Sub Saharan African People have not evolved out of the tribes and have strong tribal feelings that are a cause of concern for the betterment of these people. The Sub Saharan African Leaders have never thought of the continent as their home, despite being born here. They want to live in luxury in the Western World once their predation on the African Land cannot continue.

At present, it is poverty ridden and war torn because its people are least interested in building nations. They are more interested in butchering neighbouring tribes and wasting the resources that nature has blessed upon

Africa. Education, scientific research, economy protection and medical infrastructure is lacking in all of Africa. The deficiencies of these things have made African Population prone to disease and in the near future to decimation. With its cities in shambles, widespread loot of its natural resources and eventual pollution of its soils and waters, a very bleak future is awaiting the inhabitants of Africa. Sub Saharan Africa lacks institutions of a modern civilized democracy. Institutions are very important for running a nation in an automatic mode. These institutions were responsible for making the Western World rise above the rest of the world, because change of regime did not mean change of governance.

By 2040 AD, Sub Saharan Africa is most certain to suffer from water borne diseases and viral infections. These epidemics are going to destroy the people, if the warlords and civil unrest does not. Either civil unrest shall follow an epidemic or an epidemic shall be the cause of widespread civil unrest in Sub Saharan Africa. Africa after 2050 AD shall be a place with much less population and an easy prey for other nations. Eventually it will be under the hegemony of Corporations of the Western World supported and controlled by the Western Nations. Sub Saharan Africa shall become a thriving business interest for the Western World. It will have a lot of tourism industry and industrial enterprises, all coming from the West. Although, the African people might not receive the same cruel treatment from these corporations as they have received at the hands of their own leaders. However, a lot better conditions will prevail in Sub Saharan Africa once this time arrives. At least its children will grow in an environment without the shadow of war and death looming over the skies. Most countries in the Sub Saharan Africa will become protectorates of the Western Economy. The west shall safeguard their business interests in Africa through all means to keep peace in this part of the world.

By 2080, Western Powers shall engulf all of Sub Saharan Africa and become one big industrial estate. Slowly the mass migrations of people needed for the industries on the African Land will eventually change the demography of Sub Saharan Africa. However, it shall still be a much better place from the present days. It will be even much better from the days to come after 2040 AD when it shall suffer from the mistakes that are creations of the past and the present.

South Asia is a World in its own right, always at the receiving end in history. It has remained technologically inferior from historical times. Its population mired in all superstitions that hamper human growth and development. The Indian Sub-Continent is all that South Asia encompasses. With Pakistan, India, Bangladesh, and Sri Lanka as major nations marked on its map. Moreover, a few minor ones who share it based on culture but not the same economic importance.

This part of the planet has always had immigrations from the North during the historical times. These immigrations have come sometimes as entire tribes and at times as ravaging armies. From the times memorial the people of the South Asia have a lack of vitality. They are much averse to change and always have had a fear of the culture that thrives beyond the Hindu Kush. Especially more after the people beyond the Hindu Kush accepted Islam as their way of reaching towards God. Even historically, the Indian Armies have lacked technology in warfare. They have lacked in the art of war with no war engines, no weapons that could provide their troops with additional advantages. In addition, no military planning ever introduced into the science of war in this land mass. On whole, the Indian armies were a bunch of armed, ill-disciplined assemblies. That generally assembled in large numbers but easily dispersed by the well-drilled armies from the North. Who were much less in numbers but well trained for the battlefield.

As colony for the British Empire, it was the first time that the people of the Indian Sub- Continent had an efficient government. It prevented invasions into the Sub-Continent, provided law, and order in a lawless place. The colonial rulers laid vast infrastructure for transporting their armies and commercial goods from one place to the next. During the British Period, Indian Sub-Continent enjoyed prosperity as if it had never enjoyed in its history. Moreover, it was reaching to be at par with rest of the world, but could not because the British left.

The bane of Indian Sub-Continent's Society has been its love for faith in superstitions. Such beliefs introduced into the society many centuries ago but have not changed with the changing times. These beliefs have prevented education from reaching the people and have turned people into ignorant, mindless slaves of their ancient rituals. The Sub Continental Society still has a need for an intermediary between the men and the gods. This system of intermediaries has penetrated into the government institutions of the present Sub-Continent Governments. The governments of the Sub-Continent too have a belief like its people, that there should be an intermediary between the people and their 'ruler. In addition, this has given rise to corrupt practices in every government office, from the highest to the lowest. An efficient system, with a well-laid infrastructure that the British developed in the Indian Sub-Continent, comparable to the best in the world of those times has prematurely decayed under the self-rule of the people of the Sub-Continent.

In all of the nations of the Indian Sub-Continent, the people of this land live in an environment that turns them into weak minded, illiterate workers, meant to serve the interest of the few, in the government. The government considered as 'Sarkar', an entity that owns the people and provides them with livelihood. The people of the Sub-Continent yet have not understood the meaning of self-rule. They have a belief that it is their duty to serve those in political power. The people of the Sub-Continent believe that their survival lies in to remain servile to those who enjoy government offices. This thought lives in the mind of the 'Sahibs' or the bureaucracy too, which runs the countries of the Sub-Continent. The people of the Sub-Continent are for the disposal of the government, but the government is not for the people.

The Colonial Rulers saw the Indian Sub-Continent as a production house for raw materials to provide for the processing factories in England. They knew that an orderly system necessary to make the people of the Sub-Continent increase their production. Hence, they provided such an environment for the people. This system has deteriorated under the self-rule model run by the people of the Indian Sub-Continent.

The elected representatives and the officials think it their right to demand and accept bribes for everything that is under their authority. This attitude has sapped the strength of the Sub-Continent. The present Indian Sub-Continent is an ideal breeding ground for crony capitalism and degrading morality. As the Sub-Continent forgets its Colonial Period, its democratic institutions wither away. These institutions are slowly decaying, year after year. Until one day, no democratic institutions can remain 'viable' for the rulers of the countries outlined on the Sub-Continent. After the British Raj ended on the Indian Sub-Continent, each passing year has seen marked downfall of the democratic institutions. Each passing moment has seen the fall of its economy. Moreover, each passing decade has seen the rise of crony businesspersons and vile political forces.

The Sub-Continent has survived for so long due to the infrastructure laid by the British but that advantage will be lost. There will be no new development in social conditions, which can save the Sub-Continent from reverting to the old system, the pre-colonial system. However, there is none other to blame but the lawmakers of these countries. Who were aware of the character of their compatriots and were well aware that the system that they are creating is flawed. People making illegitimate wealth through this outdated form of governance shall hijack its entire functioning, was one major drawback of this system. This outdated bureaucratic system of governance given to the largely illiterate and ignorant population by their 'Western educated' fathers of the Constitutions, has made the bureaucracy run the Sub-Continent with utter misuse of their powers.

The system of government that is operational in the countries of the Sub-Continent gives rise to the sycophant intermediaries. The nepotistic bureaucrats and the fascist politicians too are a creation of this archaic system. The Sub-Continent's system favours big businesses. These businesses do not want the general population to compete in the industrialization of the nations in the sub-Continent. The laws enacted in the Sub-Continent, laid down for discouraging the common people to compete with established players in Industry and Commerce have proved effective in curbing industrial growth. This system gives outstanding powers to the people in government and hence serves to destroy the spirit of free enterprise.

Social justice is nearly negligible in the Sub-Continent. The populations of the countries mapped on the Sub-Continent usually have to buy justice because receiving it is a very tedious task. The police of these nations are under the direct control of political offices and hence ensure to please the rulers for selfish gains. The governments of the South Asia have ensured the courts or judiciary is understaffed in spite of the fact that they have to handle a large population. The judiciary in turn become Godly Beings, above human existence and very indifferent to the people. Those same governments have overstaffed the bureaucracy without thought. What purpose this policy has served, it is hard to understand by a person on the grounds of rationality?

A parallel economy of ill gotten, corruption generated and illegitimately gained money is a big problem for the economies of these countries. Especially since this parallel economy is the creation of very governments who are supposed to control it. This parallel economy shall remain part of the countries of the Sub-Continent. This parallel is economy is the creation of tax evaders and corruption in government offices. The money generated through this economy finds two businesses; many invest it in real estate. Others convert it into bullion and stash it in foreign banks. It is nearly impossible to trace such investments by the bureaucratic system, which is very inefficient. This economy brings no prosperity to the nations in which it runs.

With a corruption ridden bureaucracy and an unwise political class, the days for the Sub Continent are bleak in the future. The systems in these countries promote the rise of people with illegitimate gains into the corridors of power. Such crafty people have dangerous motives to decide the fate of a large population. Who they are not interested in serving but want to exploit. Such people have no love for human life, for them it is but cannon fodder or pawns of chess.

There is a big class difference among the society of the Sub-Continent. An elite VIP class, which enjoys all the privileges that the taxpayers can provide for their indulgences, is on the top of this class stratification. A working middle class, that is always at the receiving end of corrupt officials. In addition, an illiterate underprivileged class that the governments' desire were never there.

Indian Subcontinent has the most corrupt electoral system. while in some of the largest nations in the Subcontinent, not only are the politicians and the bureaucrats corrupt but the elector too is the most corrupt individual to be found anywhere on Earth. In such countries, to retain or attain high political offices it is customary and mandatory to bribe the hordes of constituents. Who vote only for those people who pay them in currency, provide free alcohol and clothing during the elections? The elector in these countries is the major cause of corruption. The voter forces the political leaders to indulge in corrupt methods to amass wealth that they have to distribute among the voters for winning elections. Due to this reason, the political leaders want to keep the majority of the population poor. So that the suffrage to sell their rights, their dignity, and their honour. For a meagre sum of money, enough to sustain them for one day the electors sell themselves.

The governments of the Sub-Continent have always blamed population pressure as the reason for their under development. They have never thought of the population as potential workers in industrial enterprises and buyers for the industrial products that can roll out of factories and fill the coffers of the state with taxes. Economic policies regarding commercial and industrial enterprises are not legislated and planned on these lines. If a free market enterprise introduced into the systems of these countries, this target achieved easily. This shall never happen due to funding that political parties receive from big business houses to maintain their monopoly.

The political parties in Indian Sub-Continent favour an illiterate majority that is easy to manipulate and easy to control. They favour a population that does not ask too many questions and believe in the propaganda spread through the media like mute spectators. Thus, the political and government offices work overtime to keep the general population of the Indian Sub-Continent poor and impoverished. Lest the people might educate their progeny and start, demanding what is rightfully theirs. They might want to share the nation's wealth and its progress. This at present is not at all reaching the common people in the Indian Sub-Continent. The middle class and the illiterate underprivileged class of the Sub-Continent shall remain trampled under the weight of the Government Officials, Politicians, and Crony Capitalists. This shall never change until the fall of this system.

By the year 2030 AD, the cities and villages of the Sub-Continent shall fill with heaps of garbage with no place to dump it. The industrial effluents shall heavily pollute the waters of the Sub-Continent. Its economy shall wither towards an end with large businesses having control over all financial institutions of the Sub-Continent. People who gained through illegitimate means will overpower every democratic institution and ultimately there shall be no social justice available in the countries of the Sub-Continent. This shall eventually lead to the downfall of the economies of the Indian Sub-Continent. Welfare of the population shall take a back seat and revenue generation policies shall prevail in these economies.

The middle class and the illiterate underprivileged class shall be at a great disadvantage due to monopolistic trade practices actively supported by each successive government. The governments shall destroy the free spirit of the people to make them servile. Some revolutionary people shall be much disgusted at this and at the point of revolt, unwilling to be servile to an unjust system. A large-scale epidemic shall first spread among the illiterate underprivileged class of the Sub-Continent. They in turn shall not have the resources for medical aid. Largely due to water borne diseases of a communicable nature, this epidemic shall spread fast among all the classes of the people. With a health system in shambles, the governments shall be in no position to contain the decimation of the population. Moreover, the population of the Sub-Continent shall come down heavily in a decade after 2030 AD.

In time, the lawlessness shall spread in the society due to monopolistic trade practices of the businesses protected by the bureaucracy and political leaders. This condition shall be responsible for a very high inflation. All infrastructures in Sub-Continent shall fall or fail. First, the energy production followed by road and rail networks will wither, that the revenue-drained governments shall not be able to upkeep and maintain. By 2050 AD, the governments of the Sub-Continent shall be at their end and shall give way to utter chaos. With weakened governments, a high inflation and lawlessness, it shall become imperative that the Sub-Continent divides into many small countries. The entire Sub Continent shall ultimately serve as a market for the factories of the West.

The Sub-Continent shall remain as a servile society. It will be exploited and abused by its rulers and never complain against the 'will of God'. Just like has happened for centuries in its history even in the present nothing has changed. By 2070 AD, the Sub-Continent like Sub Saharan Africa shall be under some sort of hegemony, enforced by the Western Economy. It shall serve as a production house of biomass raw materials for the processing plants across the world.

From all this we can judge some basic new events that shall cloud over the world by 2050 AD. While the Western and Developed Nations shall make full use of the mistakes of their ancestors and as they are trying now at present. They shall make much rectifications of their society. For making, their surroundings better suited for human life and to provide an impetus for human progress they shall provide an environment for great strides in scientific research. In addition, its innovation into technological marvels shall give much push to this world. The society of these nations, free from environmental pollution and having access to the best medical technology shall be healthy and robust. Law and order maintained with best efforts possible distinguish them apart in the present and it shall do so in the future. The Semi Developed nations might not make so great progress as the Western World or the Developed Nations. However, they shall grow and evolve much as if they are today and shall reap some of the rewards that the Developed nations will invent. On the contrary, it is a bleak future for the Eastern Countries and the Latin Americas who are not even Semi Developed.

By 2050 AD, the Third World countries shall deplete all their financial resources and it shall be deficient in the manufacture of energy. Much shortage in fuel shall exist in the Third World to transport the goods and their troops to the far corners of their countries. All that is dependent on electricity and natural carbon fuels shall suffer from the shortage of these commodities. This shall initially make other sectors suffer as well. All this mismanagement shall making living conditions pitiful for the common people while the ruling class shall not feel affected by these circumstances, at least not initially. This will give rise to insurgencies everywhere in the Third World. The mismanagement in these countries that have already been committed in the past by its population's ignorance is great. Political follies committed in these nations by their political leadership and an ignorant population are difficult to correct. These mistakes shall first make the education escape the minds of the common people. Later the health system and the infrastructure shall eventually fail. No law and order shall prevail in these nations. As law, enforcement is not functioning at present due to the policies of the ruling elite of the Third World. Very awful situation shall arise. The armed forces shall inflict all possible atrocities on their own citizens.

Due to excessive and unchecked environmental pollution, the soil and waters of these nations shall be the reasons of many diseases. All afflictions from cancer to mutated viruses shall spread among the people of the Nations that are not developed. If the citizens of these nations shall survive these calamities, malnutrition shall ensure their deaths. The cities of these nations shall suffer all the misfortunes suffered by the Medieval Europe. All conditions that led to the creation of events that made the 'Black Death' enter the lands of Europe.

In the Eastern Nations and Latin Americas, the same social conditions shall prevail as existed during the times when revolution charged the atmosphere of Europe during the early modern age. A condition of civil war shall exist but the governments of these countries shall be much prepared to use all possible force to supress any revolt by their citizens. The armed forces shall succeed in quelling the unrest by the use of the bullet and cannon ball. Nevertheless, all this upheavals shall prove fatal in the end for these nations. Finally, due to widespread disease brought about by pollution. Civil unrest and lack of infrastructure, wide scale deaths due to various afflictions, shall finally wreck devastation on the poor people living in this part of the world. Much depopulation shall commence. Just as the depopulation of many indigenous tribes in the Americas happened, from the disease the immigrating Europeans communicated that to these people. All these circumstances and misfortunes that shall befall the Third World are inevitable. Quite visible in the future due to the present conditions that are accumulating the cues for these future events are dismaying.

It is not that the Third World does not want to survive or that its people do not want to produce and increase their progeny. However, the way these people have evolved. The chemicals that make them decide on the way their governments should act. Moreover, to decide for their entire community, they cannot think about taking control of the methods that are governing these people at present. As the European Population took control over their society is impossible for these people. European common folk had taken control over its rulers and made them change for the good of all the society and not just for their own selves and their courts.

All the Western concepts that the governments of these nations practice, they do not fully implemented and neither with sincerity. While the majority in these nations are not determined to change their impending fate and have provided full support to their governments. Else, these nations shall never let such policies come into force that too by a small minority of decision makers. The population shall never remain mute electors and subjects just like their ancestors were. When the Europeans arrived on their shores and found them much lower on the scale of social development and evolution, these same conditions prevailed.

CONCLUSION OF THE 21ST CENTURY

History throughout the ages has favoured democratic forms of governments for a build-up of strong society. Democratic societies from time immemorial have taken over the authoritarian systems by force or otherwise. However, these democratic systems have always come from the Northern Hemisphere towards Southern Parts of the Globe. Whenever the Southern Authoritarian ideas have penetrated into the Northern Hemisphere's Societies, it has brought darkness and ignorance into the Northern Hemisphere. Which means that authoritarian systems are oppressive, corrupt, extinguish the flame of human spirit, and plunge the world into a dark age of ignorance.

Since Europe, that lies in the Northern Hemisphere and has a Caucasian population. European culture has flourished which has spread to other parts in the New World due to this population. If the New World were not, there Europe would have trespassed and annexed All of Africa and Asia. Just like the Czarist Russia conquered most of Central Asia up to the Borders of the Chinese Empire. All these Western Nations, which are thriving and progressing as democracies have a certain element not present in other economies. It could be possible that there could be a racial element in the evolution and practice of democratic governments, which is not the case in the darker races of Africa and Asia.

The Mongoloid Populations of the World, except the Japanese, too have a tendency not follow democratic principles of governance. Moreover, even in democratic countries of South East Asia there is a strong inclination towards authoritarian rule. It might be possible that evolution forces the Caucasian races to live in democratic societies. Because of their genetic build-up, a tendency that is not present among other racial groups, democracy is present in the Caucasian blood. Due to certain biochemical, differences that the genes have transcribed in various races of humans those differences have shown in political systems too. Different races are predisposed to live in different social organisations and forms of governments.

The cause of advancement and prosperity of the Western World, dominated by the Caucasian Population, could be that the Caucasian Human Society is evolving faster than other races. That the rate of evolution and change is more rapid in the Caucasians, maybe due to the mutations they underwent during the ice age. That made them, among other things, lighter in skin colour and varied in eye colour. In addition, this is the reason that they have also adopted a form of governance that is a mutation from the political practices adopted by other human races. This mutation could also be the reason of relative advancement of the Western World. Although no systems are perfect and in an effort to solve old issues new ones arise. New barriers for these problems' resolution are needed time after time. To overcome by evolving in a better system that can evolve along with changing challenges. These new challenges continue to create complications with each moment that takes the world into the future. Problems surmount for those who do not show the will or take part in an effort to solve the problems instead of waiting and watching the problems to resolve on their own or watch the problems make a system inoperable. Only the Western democracies have rectified and evolved according to changing times. They have built such systems that can change a little with new problems and hence these systems do not become obsolete. The Eastern political systems are on the contrary rigid and rendered obsolete in time, all will witness as one after the other, all Eastern nations fall in advance of the Western civilization.

The conclusion of the 21st century and the beginning of 22nd Century is in favour of a system that is transparent and involves its basic units, that is an individual, in to its operational mechanism. The system that provides equal opportunity to its citizens, social justice prevails in such a system. Such political systems do not trample aspirations of the people. The spirit of free enterprise and honest labour, which is essential for progress leaves from within the minds of the general population if the system becomes authoritarian. Such a system entices the decision makers into unfair and unethical methods for making gains. The authoritarian system has a tendency towards corrupt and degraded people, who rise in such a system. These are the basic principles for any system to thrive on the planet, whose most developed organism, the Homo sapiens needs for advancing farther into the evolutionary process.

If we trace the human development through the centuries, the human race had origins in the Equator and spread throughout the globe. the mutations in the Northern

Hemisphere that have taken the human civilization out of the tribal or monarchical forms of governances and introduced the idea of democracy on the planet which has failed other forms of governments. Democracy is a European concept, introduced on the planet during the European expansion and colonial rule. History has also taught us that when there was no democracy in Europe, the continent was under a 'Dark Age'. It was a time when the autocratic governance had made Europe just like to rest of the world, illiterate and ignorant.

If Europe rose to high standards of development, it was due to the advent of democracy into the European culture. It was also due to democracy that Europe was able to rule the world for a long time and due to authoritarian rule in Germany, that European Hegemony over the world ended. Democracy gave Europe the vitality to invent nationalism, in which an inhabitant of a country was part of the process to choose his government and became an integral part of system.

Due to some inherent mechanism, the Western Society evolves. The society of the Third World does not have that mechanism evolution. In addition, due to what so ever reasons this society cannot evolve but remain standing on the same place on which it stood centuries ago. As the other parts of the world could not emerge out of the dark ages after their societies not exposed to new ideas, their development was limited to the Monarchs Treasury. Once the Monarch replaced, the government changed including the state policies. It was easy for the European powers to take over these countries. As these countries did not have an established system that ran in an automatic mode.

As in Europe, where the king too was a small part of the government not its beginning and its end. Replacement of a ruler did not mean change in the system after the advent of the democratic process. Democracy was alien to the people of the Third World. Their culture not developed to run on the principles of democracy as the present indicates.

As the colonial rule period is going down into history, the democracies of the regions near the equator and those lying North and South of the Tropic of Capricorn are fast reverting to autocratic form of governments. Due to this tendency of the Eastern Economies, it is quite possible in the near future that all large nations like China and India along with the smaller nations of their kind shall suffer insurgencies. Moreover, due to their practise of governments, these large and small nations shall be broken down into smaller pieces. Their economies no longer bear the burden of artificial economy boosters that all authoritarian governments enforce to make their economies look healthy and vibrant.

All large countries in the East have a varied population, of different ethnicities and languages, held together by the earlier Local Empires or European Rulers by the force of arms because one ethnic group was stronger than the others. Within the borders of these Eastern Countries, civil unrest is always present due to infighting of populations. This unrest is weakening these countries with each passing moments as one ethnic group crushes the aspiration and rights of the other due to their outdated centralised governance.

This inherent Eastern Weakness is not present in the Western Democracies, whose population practices one religion and speaks one language. This is one of the reasons of patriotism in these countries. This holds the social fabric of these countries together, in a fairer system than the most Eastern Nations.

That the mutations caused in the Northern Hemisphere have somehow placed some humans at an advantage for practicing democracy. It has made easy for these races to live in such systems. Moreover, these humans are present in majority in the Western Nations. As far as now, democracy is the best form of government. In addition, countries that are democracies have excelled in human development. While the countries who have practised it in half or naught have not advanced with speed like democratic decentralised nations have.

All new things and social innovations that human civilization has received have passed from the Northern Hemisphere. most probably from the European Lands Southwards and Eastwards, to other cultures that have evolved outside Europe be it the Middle Eastern, South Asian, Sub Saharan or the Mongoloid Cultures. These cultures became stagnant at some particular time. Even at present, they are not willing to let go of some or most of its past social behaviours. Those behaviours did not let these societies progress in the first place. Those behaviours that make one man exploit others with immunity and with ease without providing social equality and devoid of dignity.

If the past gave advantage to the countries with democratic governments, the present has proven the superiority of democracy. Hence, the future too belongs to this form of government, undeniably. The people of the hotter regions due to some inherent physiological tendency or genetic trait cannot remain attached to democracy. They seem to favour autocracy or monarchy as a mean to promote their social needs. Wherever democracy introduced into a nation after the European Colonial Rulers left, with each passing decade the democratic institutions in these countries have reduced. Due to this, the economies of these countries have also suffered. The people of these countries shall suffer more in the days to come as all democratic aspiration remain snatched from the general population in the coming days.

As these countries finish democracy inside their borders, the pace of development in every sphere of society will slow down. Eventually these countries shall lose the race for equal share in the development of the human society. These countries shall fall back to the ancient forms of social practices that they once practised. Those practices prevalent before the Europeans established colonies all around the world and gave these nations the sweet taste of democratic rights. However, it is human to 'evolve' into a higher being and all assumptions made may prove wrong in the future. Nevertheless, that hope is but very bleak for the Third World due to past and present experiences.

The Third World Countries practice a centralized system of administration. Such systems are oppressive and eventually fall into the hands of corrupt bureaucracy and unwise political leadership. Because of the unprecedented powers, that they enjoy over the people these systems automatically promotes corruption. The governments find it easy to arm twist the population into submission. Until the population eventually rises against the system or the system falls on its own weight after decaying from wide spread corruption.

The Western Democracies favour a system that allows administration to run by towns and cities. The aspirations of the people are not hurt or suppressed in such type of administrations. People enjoy great liberty in an administration run by elected representatives who understand the needs of the people in terms of local confines. In such systems, by far the justice system is quite fair. Law and order well maintained, which is healthy for the society and the economy.

History has shown that the mutated human has come out of Europe to spread everywhere. First, this race finished the dark races that lived in the Southern parts of Europe. Slowly as these people grew in numbers, they pushed out of Europe into Asia by land routes. These same people infiltrated into North Africa through the seas. Eventually they changed much of the racial component of this part of the world. The Caucasians destroyed the Proto-Austroloid culture in Asia. Due to some political reason, the Western European culture could not spread during the Dark Ages. Nevertheless, when Renaissance permitted these people eventually penetrated into the old world of the east and the new worlds of the Americas and Australia. Just as this culture is dominant in the new world, it would have happened in the old world. If the Great wars had not occurred, one by one all Eastern nations and their populations would have given in to the Western people. The west would have easily consumed or assimilated these people into its culture. In fact, the Two Great Wars in Europe saved the Eastern nations from complete extinction. However, the west is slowly recovering from the shock of the great wars. At the same time, the east is dying a slow death inflicted upon itself by its own people.

The Western Civilization will spread into the Latin American Continent in a big way after 2050 AD. After the epidemics created by widespread decimate the Latin American population. The continent shall shelter a large population of immigrants from the Western Nations. Later on after 2070 AD, Sub Saharan Africa too will be part of Western Civilization. This continent will depopulate by widespread disease and human neglect. This will bring the east and the west in direct conflict after centuries of hibernation, after the crusades.

Finally, in the beginning of the 22nd Century, the west shall advance in the Middle East using its military might. The Middle Eastern people, already weakened by conflicts and ignorance shall easily give in to the military advances of the Western military might.

For a moment, the West will take a respite on the borders of Central Asia. The Russian Federation, the Central Asian nations and South Asia will serve as a buffer between the west and the Mongoloid world. First, the Western armies will take South Asia, after this brief respite is over. Slowly the Western Civilization shall penetrate into the Mongoloid World. This too world be weakened by its authoritarian political system to take on the Western might. Finally, by the end of 22nd Century, the Western form of government shall represent the entire planet. Caucasian population will be the dominant human race on this planet when this happens. All other races will have minor traces, that too within the dominant Caucasian population that will survive into the 23rd Century.

The purpose of life on Earth is to evolve through ebbs of time to become better suited for challenges that thrown at it from all the natural barriers that put in place by nature to end a species' existence. Moreover, the various societies that form the human the species are no different. If the races or societies consisting of humans shall become stagnant and not evolve, that society or race will lose its foothold on the land beneath its feet. The majority of it shall be lost and the survivors assimilated into whichever race or society that shall, have the capacity and the capability to evolve through the ages by devising new mechanisms and thoughts that can bring change.

The Homo sapiens neanderthalensis lost the race of evolution to the modern humans because it was not fit to survive in the changing environment of the globe. It lost to humans due to, most possibly, the mounting competitive pressures that it was receiving from its newly evolved cousin, Homo sapiens. The other reasons could have been climatic changes or natural catastrophes. Nevertheless, if the first two reasons were the cause of the extinction of the Neanderthal Man. the social setup of the African and Asian Societies, including their political leaders and decision makers should realize that if corrective measures not devised to fill the faults in their societies and governments, that end is awaiting them as well.

One day the societies in the sphere of Western Democracies and the nations like Japan shall one day reach such level of sophistication and advancement that the other forms of governments shall become extinct. Such authoritarian governments and political ideas are already damaging the cause of a progressive society for man. However, once, as these governments and societies, have started to lag behind the Western World and mismanaged economically and socially, they shall never recover. Ultimately, these economies or societies will meet the fate of the Neanderthal man. The populations who support and live in such setups shall meet that fate as well. Because survival is harsh in this world and nature does not favour those who are weak and sickly.

The Eastern World has examples of some high characters and personalities with vision. They have given up their luxuries, their choices, and their families for the betterment of the society. Nevertheless, all the sacrifices that these individuals have made have come to a naught because neither the Eastern Leadership nor the Eastern Population have learned or applied the altruistic and progressive thinking of such liberty loving, dignified people. People who wanted the Eastern World to shed their ignorance and make all people in their midst enjoy the fruit of human civilization are not appreciated in a society full of bigotry and prejudice.

Hence, the future belongs to the Western Democratic Economies. These economies are developing at a great pace. The Eastern Economies shall never outpace these economies, for a long time or maybe never in the history of humans. Eventually a society that is much developed and socially evolved has mightier military muscle to take over the less 'evolved' culture. It also takes control over the resources that nature has provided on this planet. It also has the mind to use these resources according to its wishes. That shall eventually happen when the Western Economy is in a position to do so. This shall happen 'inevitably'.